Pak Mei Kung Fu

Martial Concepts

&

Training Methods

Pak Mei Kung Fu

Martial Concepts

&

Training Methods

白眉派 拳理 練功

紐約白眉拳術文化保會
NEW YORK CITY

Williy Pang

TNP Multimedia LLC

Pak Mei Kung Fu: Martial Concepts & Training Methods

TNP Multimedia LLC
P.O. Box 130197
New York, NY 10013

Book Design by Mary Chiu.

Disclaimer:
The author, assistants, and publisher of this work and material are NOT RESPONSIBLE in any manner whatsoever for any injury which may occur through reading or following the material and/or instructions in this work.
The material and activities, physical or otherwise, described in this work may be too strenuous or dangerous for some people, and the reader(s) should consult a physician before engaging in them.

ISBN 978-0-9814813-2-6

First Edition

Printed in the United States of America

For 美莉 and 俊興

A NOTE ABOUT ROMANIZATION

The English equivalent of Chinese names and terms is quite often confusing due to the various dialects which are prevalent throughout China in conjunction with the occasional non-standardized Romanization of such names and terms in written form.

With the exception of the name *Pak Mei* and some proper names which have been preserved in their Wade-Giles translations (such as *Shaolin*) or other conventions to maintain their established methods of expression, the Chinese names and terms in this book will utilize a modified version of the Yale system of Cantonese to facilitate a close approximation to what the terms should sound like when enunciated in the Cantonese dialect. In this modification, the letter "h" will not be used as a tone indicator as it has been established in the Yale system.

Some terms, such as *Emei*, will be kept in their Pinyin format since they are the most familiar conventions in which most readers are accustomed to seeing.

It should be noted that the official Yale system's Cantonese written standard of the name Pak Mei is actually *Baahk Meih*.

INTRODUCTION

Pak Mei Kung Fu is considered a *traditional* Chinese martial art, meaning that it was structured in a manner that was typical of martial instruction prior to the establishment of the People's Republic of China on October 1, 1949. The development of discipline and self-defense through conditioning and drills, prearranged fighting routines, and cooperative partnered practice was the standard training methodology of many martial practitioners throughout China regardless of style or system. This fundamental program provided one with a sense of empowerment and emphasized the importance of efficient and effective practical implementation, particularly during the times when these strengths were needed most for sheer survival.

Within the contemporary context, this classical curriculum and traditional training approach serves as a foundational starting point, advocating a code of commitment and conveying a set of values and etiquette that aims to elevate the individual and improve our now global society. It presents the practitioner with a platform to be a lifelong devotee by balancing the different stages and personal requirements of one's life: vigorous training and discipline during the vitality of youth leading to a keen awareness and technical refinement in one's martial mid-life, and ultimately providing the practitioner with the clarity and calmness expressed by the harmonious union of the body, mind, and spirit throughout old age.

As styles and systems are passed on from one generation to the next, each respective art form experiences an inevitable evolution with regard to personal preferences, environmental influences, and the technological advancements of the times. However, the uniqueness of each style is maintained through its founding precepts and guiding principles. Without such defining and distinguishing characteristics, there is an absence of the art and the most effective techniques merely become categorized within a catalog of generic street-fighting tactics.

To this end, it is of the utmost importance that the traditional principles and essential core of Pak Mei Kung Fu are maintained for the sake of posterity within the wide expanse of ever-evolving combative arts.

Pak Mei, or White Eyebrow, is both a martial folk icon and a system of self-defense. As a prominent figure in Southern Chinese martial arts, Pak Mei has typically been portrayed as a formidable pugilist. As a martial art, Pak Mei was organized into a fighting system by Master Cheung Lai Chuen during the early part of the 20th Century in Guangdong, China. The allure of the art generally stems from the powerful impressions established by these two particular name associations.

The concepts, principles, summaries, and training methodologies presented in this work are intended to serve as *one* source of information – not *the* source of instruction. It is designed to provide a point of reference, inspire self-reflection, encourage dialogue, and promote a spirit of further inquiry and self-cultivation.

Authentic Kung Fu is a process.

It truly is about the *hard work* that one is willing to put in to achieve the ultimate skill of becoming a quality human being.

Train hard. Be well.

Respectfully,

Williy Pang

August, 2011

~ TABLE OF CONTENTS ~

張家白眉派

宗師張禮泉

Grandmaster Cheung Lai Chuen

張炳森　　　張炳林　　　張炳發

Master　　　Master　　　Master

Cheung Bing Sam　Cheung Bing Lam　Cheung Bing Faat

CHAPTER ONE

Foundations of Martial Power

"If you work at the parts the whole will be a success."

- Unknown

Pak Mei Kung Fu was devised as a fighting system based upon a combative tenet of maximized effectiveness through minimal exertion – better known as efficiency. Throughout all martial arts, regardless of country of origin or individual emphasis, the apex of the art is to achieve this martial status. To this end, Pak Mei Kung Fu shares the exact same aim. However, it is the uniqueness by which this is achieved in Pak Mei that distinguishes it from its martial kin.

This section will examine the foundational concepts, principles, and platforms of martial power defined within the scope of Pak Mei Kung Fu.

Pak Mei Kung Fu: The Internal Art

In Chinese, Pak Mei Kung Fu has always been classified within the category of *noi ga* (內家), or internal family of martial arts. Before Master Cheung Lai Chuen (宗師張禮泉) organized the finest elements of all which he had learned during his youth: Wanderers' Style (流民派; *Lau Man Paai*), Li Family (李家; *Lei Ga*), and Dragon Style (龍形; *Lung Ying*), into a single system called Pak Mei Paai (白眉派), he was immersed in an art obscurely dubbed *Emei Shaolin* (峨眉少林; *Ngo Mei Siu Lam* in Cantonese) referencing the well-known reputations of *Mount Emei's* internal emphasis and *Shaolin's* fighting methods that would ultimately revolutionize his martial material.

While the term *internal* has assumed a more philosophical position and holistic angle during this current era of Chinese martial arts due to much scholarly discourse, the concept of internal was viewed somewhat differently within the fighting framework of certain schools of pugilism particularly during the early part of the 20th Century in China. The combative context in which the term internal was used within this setting was very simple and straightforward – having the proper alignment and integrated structure to maximize one's martial techniques. It was a concept used to differentiate pure athleticism from ergonomic optimization, or absolute brawn as opposed to a refined expression of martial power achieved by way of whole-body synchronization, respectively. Within this perspective, Pak Mei Kung Fu is indeed an internal martial art.

However, as a highly developed view of internal began to emerge with the assimilation and elaboration of Taoist meditative and medical methodologies, a line of demarcation was drawn between the fighting styles that incorporated these practices and those that did not. As a result, the paradigms of internal and external martial arts were revised and roughly defined. Styles which subscribe to a foundation of unified body movement, a physical state of dynamic relaxation, and a calm and clear fighting frame of mind were deemed internal arts. Fighting approaches that rely upon sequential or segmented body actions, physical strength and speed, and lethal intent – *saat hei* (殺氣), were grouped together into the arena of external arts. Within this schema, Pak Mei would fit perfectly into neither designation.

As a result, it would be more appropriate to classify Pak Mei Kung Fu as a hybrid art, blending the external execution of martial power with an internal emphasis on its expressive manifestation.

At this point, it is purposeful to identify the definition of martial power and to examine the features essential to its uniqueness within Pak Mei Kung Fu.

Ging: A Comprehensive Concept

In the scientific world of physics, the terms energy, power, work, and force maintain very distinct technical formulas and definitions. However, these same words are used quite loosely and nearly interchangeably in the realm of Chinese martial arts. For the purposes of this text, the liberally interpreted rather than scientific form of these words will be used to convey points pertaining to martial principles and expressions of power. While there may be a scientific premise for that which will be discussed, such explanations are beyond the scope of this work.

Within Pak Mei Kung Fu, *ging* (勁) is a complex connotative term used to refer not only to martial power, but to all phases of issuing force. Ging, in essence, refers to the performance of an action without a sole reliance upon physical strength throughout the entire course of the movement. When only *lik* (力), sheer muscular strength, is utilized throughout the entirety of movements: *qi* (氣) – intrinsic energy (to be discussed later in detail), increases and builds in the muscles of the area where the work occurs; tension and stiffness arise as a result, obstructing the fluid flow of qi; fatigue sets in quicker; and gains through muscular exertion are typically short-term. Conversely, when ging is exercised: tendons and ligaments are emphasized in the extremities, thereby assisting the initial muscular action of the movement and assuming more of the work throughout the entirety of the motion; relaxation and reduced muscular stress occurs as a result, facilitating a smooth and continuous transport of qi that properly energizes the organs and extremities; physical endurance is raised; and more physical productivity is achievable.

In addition to the aforementioned ideas, the essential elements of yi and qi must be addressed to further a thorough discussion of ging. *Yi* (意) is the actively intelligent mind – it governs the body's actions and processes intent. With regard to ging, yi must lead qi – in this case, the body's intrinsic energy force, to support

4

the areas where ging will be manifested. Initially, the mind leads this intrinsic energy force to invigorate the muscles of an area, thereby maximizing the muscles' efficiency. As the muscles grow more capable, there is less stress and tension in them which enables qi to flow more effectively. Eventually with prolonged training, the muscles function so optimally that the tendons at the extremes of the muscles assume the majority of the workload. As qi flows fluidly through the muscles, it also energizes and sustains the adjoining tissues, globally strengthening the individual's physiology. Hence, when: minimal lik is used, qi no longer needs to be consciously led by yi, and maximum force or power is attained, ging is achieved.

Lik and Ging: A Comparative Survey

To further illustrate the differences between lik and ging, consider the activities of two distinct professions, that of a professional mover and those of a professional baseball pitcher. While the mover typically uses lik, the pitcher characteristically utilizes ging, respectively. A professional mover carrying and maneuvering bulky and awkward furniture must constantly draw upon muscular strength to support and control the load. The heavier the workload becomes, aside from careful planning and strategic maneuvering, the more emphasis is placed upon the muscles. For a pitcher, each hurl of the ball employs the precise coordination of planting the push-off leg, turning the hip, chambering the arm, accelerating and slinging the arm, releasing the ball, and following through the direction of the throw. In this scenario, the synchronized body mechanics of the pitcher enables the individual to release an enormous amount of focused force into a single crisp action. Since there is minimal tension of the muscles involved, the pitching action can be exercised repeatedly until the individual eventually exhausts the body's ability to optimally perform the motion.

From the points that have been presented, the following impressions aptly outline the association between lik and ging:

- Lik employs strength; ging utilizes force: lik is dependent upon the might of muscles rather than the coordinated efforts of accompanying tissues, correct body positioning, and supportive qi that is characteristic of ging.

- Lik is limited; ging is comprehensive: for the most part, when actions involve muscles only, the areas that are typically overworked are the arms, the back, or the legs – essentially the large muscle group areas. Stress and strain in these areas can lead to injury. When movements involve a more collaborative and coordinated effort from supportive tissues such as tendons and ligaments, the workload is balanced among a broader range of body parts, thereby maximizing efficiency and energy output.

- Lik is observable; ging is invisible: the action and intensity of muscular exertion is viewable – bulging biceps when curling a barbell filled with weights. The instantaneous discharge of ging is less measurable – qi that rushes throughout an individual's body reacting to having been accidentally struck with the tip of a lit cigarette.

- Lik is blunt and dull; ging is sudden and sharp: muscular strength is rather firm and rigid compared to the lively and abrupt emission of ging.

- Lik is rudimentary power; ging is a refined form of energy emission: lik is a basic approach to performing any physical action – muscles are used. It should not be mistaken to be ineffective, but it should be noted that it is a less efficient form of martial power. Ging, on the other hand, needs to be trained and developed. While some individuals may have a natural aptitude for its acquisition, ging still needs to be nurtured and cultivated over the course of the practitioner's martial pursuits.

In Pak Mei Kung Fu, the goal is to transform initial lik to advanced ging by training the body's intrinsic energy to support the individual's internal physiology and external physique which will in turn effectively maximize one's martial power.

In the subsequent expositions, ging will be used to refer to the *san faat* (身法), or body methods, behind the production of force and the manner and motion in which the force can be executed. While each concept covers a unique aspect of ging, each feature is inseparable from the other as ging is executed in Pak Mei Kung Fu.

Luk Ging: The 6 Sectors of Kinetic Bridging

Luk ging (六勁), or literally the six forces, refers to the 6 critical areas of the body that are identified as the key zones that activate the proper production and execution of ging in Pak Mei Kung Fu. Without compromising the underlying principle of whole body coordination and integrated force emission, these six areas have been defined differently within the diverse Pak Mei lineages. For example, Cheung Bing Lam (張炳林) – Cheung Lai Chuen's second son, classified luk ging as: *geuk* (腳; legs), *yiu* (腰; waist), *fuk* (腹; abdomen), *bok* (膊; shoulders), *sau* (手; hands), and *geng* (頸; neck), while Cheung Bing Faat (張炳發) – Cheung's third son, determined that the six areas should be: *geuk, yiu, bok, sau, geng,* and *nga* (牙; teeth).

Within many Hong Kong-based lineages, the six sectors accountable for the physical aspect of generating force are: *ma* (馬; stance), *yiu* (腰; waist), *bui* (背; back), *sau* (手; hands), *geng* (頸; neck), and *nga* (牙; teeth). Their synchronous collaboration facilitates the optimum force that can be generated and issued within a Pak Mei technique. Each sector contributes to the continuum of force production by bridging or linking the significant portions of the body from the ground upward to complete the kinetic circuit. When an area successfully connects with the succeeding sector, the bridge by which the force travels is properly formed. For instance, when the stance is firmly rooted, the waist is able to receive and direct the force drawn from the stance. Conversely, should an area fail to sync properly with its counterparts, the force will be greatly compromised as a result of the improper bridging of the body's key components. For

8

example, if a punch is thrown before the stance is properly rooted, the force behind that punch will be minimal or even nonexistent. In this case, the power of the punch came from the sheer muscular action of the arm (lik) rather than the coordinated efforts of the entire body (ging).

This section will further examine the function of each sector of the body responsible for the principle of luk ging.

Pak Mei Ma: Foundation and Footwork

The *Pak Mei ma* (白眉馬), literally the Pak Mei horse, is the name of the primary stance that Pak Mei practitioners employ. The poetic phrase *ding bat ding, baat bat baat* (丁不丁, 八不八) – person, not person; eight, not eight, depicts the positioning of the feet which will support the Pak Mei stance, one that is a cross between the pigeon-toed stance where both feet are angled inward along the same latitude and the classical bow stance where the width of the foundation is more elongated. Within this hybrid structure, the body's center of gravity is lowered enough to provide a firm root balancing the weight of the upper body between both legs while the practitioner's mobility and agility are not compromised as a result of a stance that is neither too rigid nor slow in response to the practitioner's reactions.

In order for the Pak Mei ma to exist, certain physical conditions must be met:

- With regard to the feet: the toes must grip the ground; the heels must press into the earth; and the hollow of each foot, the arch and the center, must avoid contact with the floor. The clutching toes and depressing heels allow for a firm root while the hollow of the arches enables flexibility and mobility. The tenacious action of the toes and heel enables the energy or force to be drawn upward through the stance and to the waist. Furthermore, this foot shape facilitates the optimal contraction and release of ging that is coordinated with the rest of the body. The minimal contact that the surface area of the foot has with the ground provides opportunities for quicker movement and fluid footwork. Shifting, pivoting, and stepping motions are smoother and swifter as a result of the raised arch's arc.

- The legs must be slightly bent at the knees and properly aligned with the feet and the waist. They provide balance by supporting and stabilizing the practitioner's entire structure, and function as the conduit through which the force travels from the lower extremities to the waist and onto the trunk and limbs of the upper body.

- The kwa (胯), the pectineus muscles that adduct the thighs and flex the hip joint, must be flexible yet firm. The closing of the kwa stabilizes the practitioner's stance and guards the groin area. The opening of the kwa regulates the range of the Pak Mei practitioner's attacking and counter-maneuvering footwork.

- The coccyx, or tailbone, must be slightly positioned inward to assist the fluidity of qi flow and the release of ging. Its inward curve should neither be overemphasized nor disregarded. The incorrect positioning of the tailbone can result in a structural imbalance or inadequate circulation of qi, respectively.

It is important to note that the Pak Mei ma is a training stance designed to acclimate and assist the practitioner with the proper posture that the legs must maintain to effectively achieve ging. When the practitioner reaches a stage of true mastery, the legs will be able to successfully issue ging regardless of the positioning of the stance.

Yiu: The Power of the Waist

In any system, style or family method of Chinese martial arts, the stance is considered the root of raw power and the waist action is considered the source of refined and directed force behind any technique or action. The *yiu* (腰), or waist, in this context not only refers to the individual's waistline, but encompasses the width of the frontal area just above the hip bone and below the rib cage, and the lumbar region of the back. Typically known as the core, this band of area around the body is responsible for acting as the fulcrum between the lower and the upper sections of the body, managing alignment, maintaining the body's global balance, and leading the ging that will be issued.

The proper configuration of the stance with the upper sectors of the body is achieved through a stable and supple connection with the yiu. Stances are secured by a firm waist; fluid footwork is accompanied by a flexible one. As stances combine with stepping patterns, the waist adjusts to maintain the body's equilibrium. A posture change must be coordinated in conjunction with appropriate waist movement; furthermore, skilled waist rotation enables seamless transitions of sophisticated footwork that support both advantageous body positioning and intricate hand techniques found in Pak Mei methods.

The waist region is also responsible for processing and directing the force that is drawn upward from the stance and conveying it to the other sectors of the body. Within the waist region lies what is considered the source of qi and the foundation of force discharge – the *dan tian* (丹田; *daan tin* in Cantonese). This energy center, literally the cinnabar field, is located approximately three finger-widths below the navel. Qi is cultivated and harnessed in the dan tian and circulated throughout the body to energize the viscera and extremities. The rotary motion of the dan tian leading the articulation of the waist enables ging to manifest throughout the body. The contraction and release of qi in the dan tian translates to force that is guided by the waist action's directional command to the other sectors of the body. Lateral, vertical, and angular motions are dictated by the turning and twining of the waist. The combination of a mindfully nurtured dan tian and a properly trained waist ensures the correct execution of ging in a Pak Mei technique.

Bui: Back Strength

The back is one of the most important yet misrepresented aspects of Pak Mei Kung Fu. The *bui* (背) consists of the lumbar and thoracic vertebrae of the spine; and, the external obliques, latissimus dorsi, teres major, teres minor, and trapezius muscles of the back. In its entirety, the bui is responsible for proper posture and alignment, connecting the stance and waist to the torso and extremities. It is the upper channel through which martial force travels within the body prior to manifesting martial ging.

The lumbar and thoracic sections of the spine, the lower and middle back, respectively, maintain their natural upright alignment, supporting the neck and head while balancing the upper body with its lower counterpart. The structural stability of an upright spine ensures a sense of integrated balance by preventing shifts or deviations from the body's central axis. Additionally, it serves to fix the location of the body's center of gravity at the dan tian which is the ideal balance point that will maximize the efficacy of intricate movements without sacrificing stability. When the torso is out of alignment, the individual will typically try to compensate for the imbalance by shifting in some manner, even perhaps to the point of hunching, in order to regain an impression of stability. This improper positioning can lead to poor posture as well as the increased risk of injury from the overuse of other body parts to offset the unevenness in the body structure.

The flexibility of the back facilitates the concaving of the thoracic cavity, or chest area, creating the posture technically called *haam hung* (陷胸) – sunken chest, and provincially known as *hau hung* (猴胸), or monkey's chest. This structure serves to dissipate the direct impact of an oncoming attack as well as to extend the length of the practitioner's strikes and supporting offensive maneuvers. As the external obliques, latissimus dorsi, teres major, teres minor, and trapezius muscles flex, the shoulders shift slightly forward and create a rounding effect. Subsequently, the structural arch formed by the chest acts as a brace against an opponent's attacks, diminishing the full force of an incoming strike and reducing the prospect of personal injury from the attack. This employs the same notion of the tuck position that is used defensively by Western boxers. The round shape can receive the energy of an incoming punch and disperse it throughout the entire structure rather than let the full brunt of a blow immobilize a defending arm or body part. On occasions this has been interpreted as absorbing an attack; however, the Pak Mei practitioner's techniques serve to repulse and redirect a blow rather than absorb the energy and force of the impact.

Proper spinal alignment also enables the extension of strikes which is of utmost importance in the effectiveness of close range techniques. The simultaneous action of blocking and striking, or even striking and striking, requires the structural stability afforded by an upright spine. An unbalanced upper body, particularly during the execution of techniques can lead to unstable

14

and inaccurate strikes as well as uncoordinated and insufficient support from all of the critical sectors of the body.

Sau: Hands-On Applications

Sau (手), or the hand, actually encompasses all of the sections of the arm from the shoulders to the tips of the fingers. Within this network of force producing sectors in the body, the hands are of primary importance. They are the extremities most responsible for regulating contact with the opponent, manipulating techniques, and emitting force.

Within Pak Mei Kung Fu, the sau, or arm – typically known as *kiu* (橋), or bridge, in Chinese martial arts, is divided into three segments: the shoulder, the elbow, and the wrist. These hubs of articulation are the key sites that enable the force to travel from the stance, waist and back to the arms and the hands. Ging that is issued through the arms can be greatly reduced due to improper positioning, hitches in the joints, or misjudgment in range. On the other hand, these are target areas to attack on the opponent's body for the same reasons that ging cannot be ideally emitted through the arms of a practitioner.

The shoulders, *bok* (膊), need to be relaxed and even. Tension in the shoulder areas reduces the ability for qi to properly transfer to the extremities. A raised shoulder creates a structural imbalance and a shift in the body's central center of gravity at the dan tian; a pair of raised shoulders, as in a shrug, restricts breathing to the

15

thoracic cavity rather than at the dan tian, again minimizing qi circulation. Slightly forward shoulder shifts are the result of chest cavity changes assisted by upright spinal support. The shoulders remain level with the aid of the other sectors of the body, thereby providing a unified execution of force in Pak Mei techniques.

The elbows are aimed at the earth, better known as *chong jau/jang* (藏肘), or concealed elbows, and kept close to the body. They are ideally positioned when they are aligned with the knees. As a defensive strategy, a bent elbow can retract quickly in response to a visceral attack. No matter how fast a practitioner's reactions may be, the tools required to carry out the response need to be in place. As a matter of offense, sunken elbows provide the physics of leverage to support a practitioner's techniques. An elbow outside the practitioner's body width may compromise the practitioner's integrated attack utilizing all of the sectors of the body. Retracted elbows facilitate faster chained sequences of simultaneous offensive and defensive maneuvers, forcing an opponent into an uncomfortable and unfavorable position. With regard to maximizing qi circulation, the lowering of the elbows lowers the qi, thereby sinking and returning it to the dan tian. In contrast, elbows that have a wide flair outside of the body's borders elevate the practitioner's qi to the upper portion of the body. When this occurs, qi circulation is unproductive and its potency is hampered.

The hands complement each other – acting simultaneously when techniques are executed. As one hand defends, the other attacks. As one attacks, the other assists. There are no useless movements or empty moments in Pak Mei techniques. Levels of contact vary only in the manner in which the emphasis is communicated by the teacher. The arms engage with intent and attack with one specific objective – to end the conflict triumphantly. Within Pak Mei Kung Fu, there are several hand formations that are employed:

- *ping cheui* (平槌) – level punch (standard fist)

- *fung ngaan cheui* (鳳眼槌) – phoenix-eye punch (standard fist with a protruding knuckle of the index finger)

- *biu ji* (鏢指) – thrusting/pointing fingers

- *jeung* (掌) – palm

- *jaau* (爪) – claw

Within the palm and claw formations, there are further permutations in each category. For instance, with regard to grabs, there are *fu jaau* (虎爪) and *ying jaau* (鷹爪), tiger and eagle claws, respectively. The subtleties are found in both the physical formations of the claws and their respective applications.

In general, the Pak Mei practitioner's hand skills seek to control, maneuver around, and penetrate through the opponent's offensive movements and defensive guard. Synchronized sectors of the body support the handwork in a collaborative effort to issue ging into the techniques. While a practitioner's *sau faat* (手法), or hand methods, may be exemplary, it is the ging which makes them effective.

Geng: Coordinating and Conditioning the Neck

The neck, or *geng* (頸), is responsible for connecting the head with the trunk of the body, transporting air into the body's respiratory system, and sheltering the carotid artery – the main supply route of blood to the head. The series of cervical vertebrae of the spine provide the structural support of the neck.

In Pak Mei Kung Fu, the neck is considered a major area of articulation, meaning it has multidirectional rotation and maintains a degree of flexibility within the limits of the spine. As one of the six sectors of force production, it is important that the neck is held upright and firm. The ging that is generated by the body can be so forceful and abrupt that, without strength and stability in this area, injuries to the neck such as whiplash can occur. It is critical that attention and awareness is paid to this particular region.

The contraction and release of ging that takes place in the body corresponds to the tension and relaxation of the neck muscles, respectively. This action promotes *hau ging* (喉勁), or throat strength, ideally developing the neck muscles to become impervious to strikes. In the event that a technique fails to defend the neck sufficiently, the expectation is that hau ging, that is a product of luk ging, will be able to repel the attack and preserve the throat area.

An additional safeguard pertaining to throat protection is the posture known as *chin tau* (千頭) – one thousand character head. This phrase describes the tucked chin position that mimics the downward slope of the Chinese character for 1,000. This defensive posture minimizes the size of the throat area that can be openly vulnerable during altercations. Again, this protective pose is similar to the one employed by the Western boxer.

The throat requires precautionary and mindful measures for its protection. The experienced and knowledgeable practitioners will instinctively guard and upkeep the development of this area. Beginners must continually work to internalize the importance of defending this area.

Nga: Teeth Gritting Closure

The final link in the process of producing force in Pak Mei Kung Fu is the teeth, or *nga* (牙). To grasp the role that the teeth play within this physiological network, one can envision the body as an electrical circuit grid. While this analogy will have its limitations, the points to be made about luk ging can be conveyed in a more tangible manner.

An electric circuit has three primary components: voltage, current and resistance. Electricity needs a source, such as a battery. This is comparable to the combination of the dan tian internally, and the body's stance and waist action externally. The battery delivers a voltage, similar to the idea of pressure. Voltage in the case of luk ging can be compared to qi. The voltage forces a current to flow throughout the wires in the circuit – the same way that qi travels throughout the body from the dan tian to the viscera to the extremities. If there is a break in the circuit, the current will be disrupted, disabling the flow of the current to the other wires in the circuit. When the current is continuous throughout the circuit, it causes things to work such as lighting a light bulb. The devices that make use of the current are called the load. The release of force through the extremities or other body parts can be considered the load since it is making use of the bio-current or qi. It is important to note that the load and the wires in an electric circuit are in opposition, or resist, the flow of the current, either making it weaker or diminishing it completely. This is known as resistance. As a final note with regard to an electric circuit, the better the conducting materials are in the circuit, the better the quality of the flow. Hence, the more relaxed and conditioned the body is, the better the qi flow and the greater the ging.

Within luk ging, as each sector connects with the next, the force is able to travel in a lively and dynamic manner. The teeth are the final connection, joining the mandible with the maxilla – the lower and upper jaw, respectively. The formation of a solid and stable connection in these bones enables the head to receive, circulate and disperse the ging produced by the body in a constructive and harmless manner. In this case, a closed jaw acts as a conductor and a disconnected jaw acts as a resistor.

This concept is akin to power-lifters who clench their teeth during the peak of the lift – many have resorted to using a mouth guard to cushion the impact of the clench. A solid connection provides a solid, clean lift. Conversely, loose connections lose energy through the jaw as a result of energy that escapes from the unconnected area in the bio-circuit. When a technique is executed in Pak Mei Kung Fu, the surge of force is typically sudden and sharp. The clasping of the jaws also serves to disperse the shock of the force rather than to absorb it in the head when the jaws are open. Such force without reinforcement or bracing mechanisms can lead to possible damage to blood vessels, nerve endings, the eyes, and even the brain in the long term.

An additional feature of the clench is to secure the tongue in both a safe and functional position. As previously stated, while one executes a Pak Mei technique the force is ideally and intentionally sudden and sharp. A tongue kept within the mouth's cavity avoids being accidentally bitten during the release of ging. Reactions do not always take into consideration the safety of every single body part. In this case, a reaction or release of ging can be so sudden and instinctive that the tongue may not be able to retract quickly enough to escape the teeth's clenching action – should one have a tendency to dangle the tongue between the teeth or outside the mouth.

In terms of harmonizing the body's physiology, keeping the tongue against the upper palate activates the parasympathetic nervous system and stimulates saliva production. As the tongue bridges the inside of the upper and lower jaw, the rest of the body's rhythmic movements, specific breathing patterns, and meditative focus work in unison to switch on the parasympathetic nervous system, the part of the autonomic nervous system that counteracts the physiological effects of the sympathetic nervous system by slowing the heart rate, signaling digestive secretions, constricting the pupils, and dilating the blood vessels. In other words, it calms the body down. The saliva plays an important role in indicating that the body is properly hydrated and in sanitizing the inside of the mouth. Lysozyme, an anti-bacterial enzyme, is found in saliva and contributes to cleansing the oral cavity while the tongue adjoins the upper and lower portions of the jaw.

Within the context of Traditional Chinese Medicine (TCM) and qigong theory, keeping the tongue on the upper palate of the mouth completes the path of qi circulation known as Small Heavenly Circulation (小週天 : *siu jau tin* in Cantonese; *xiao zhou tian* in Mandarin). The body is divided into two main energy channels: *yam mak* (任脈; *ren mai* in Mandarin) and *duk mak* (督脈; *du mai* in Mandarin). Yam mak, known as the Conception Channel, manages yin circulation. It begins at the lower palate of the mouth, travels down the median of the front of the body, and concludes at the point between the legs known as *wui yam* (會陰; *hui yin* in Mandarin). Duk mak, or the Governing Channel, directs yang circulation. It initiates from the wui yam point, moves up along the spine, travels over the crown of the head, and ends at the upper palate of the mouth. The Conception and Governing Channels are joined when the tongue rests on the upper palate, completing this energy circulation circuit called the Small Heavenly Circulation. This facilitates qi circulation throughout the entire body and qi regulation to the internal organs. Fortified qi flow throughout the entire body including the extremities and internal organs is known as Great Heavenly Circulation (大週天: *daai jau tin* in Cantonese; *da zhou tian* in Mandarin).

Sei Noi Biu Ging: The 4 Internalized Dynamic Forces

Sei noi biu ging (四內標勁) refers to the four internal features of issuing force in Pak Mei Kung Fu used to collectively express a set of essential criteria for the effective execution of techniques in close range combat. Within this context, the four primary characteristics of sei noi biu ging: *tan, tou, fau,* and *cham,* serve as descriptors detailing how ging should be experienced, produced and exerted by a Pak Mei practitioner.

The Figurative Language of Sei Noi Biu Ging

Tan (吞) – literally meaning to swallow, represents the idea of ingesting the force of an enemy's attack in a manner that neutralizes the threat and compromises his stability. When the practitioner redirects the power of an adversary's punch, dissipates the energy of an incoming kick, resists attempts at joint manipulation, or withstands the effort to be thrown, tan is the principle that enables these actions to take place. The inward action of swallowing directs the energy of an attack toward the practitioner's foundation and into the ground to hinder the technique and unbalance the opponent. It is an aspect of close range counterattacking supported by the practitioner's integrated body and breathing mechanics, positional advantage, technical skill, and unrelenting intent.

Tou (吐) – to spit, conveys to the practitioner that techniques, when executed, must surge outward both instinctually and lively. As the combative complement to tan, tou is the discharging state of techniques. The energy of all the practitioner's movements originates from a stable stance, amplifies as it transfers through the body's core, and is refined throughout the different sections of the upper extremities: the shoulders, elbows, and hands. This enables the body to act as one comprehensive unit, strengthening the force behind the fighting tactics that utilize short concentrated power. While the opponent recovers from being drawn in by the vigor of the swallowing dynamic, the practitioner's counter capitalizes on the weakened stage of the opponent's engagement.

Fau (浮) – or float, alludes to a state of relaxation similar to what is required to remain adrift on a body of water. Relaxation in this case is defined by the absence of both tension in the muscles and stiffness of the joints. Martially, fau is perceived as a phase of movement when the force of a technique is able to travel in an unobstructed path throughout the practitioner's body until it is ready to be released. It can be considered the interval where energy is gathered prior to its discharge and restored following the execution of the technique. However, relaxation should not be misinterpreted as being limp or weightless. On the contrary, fau maintains a quality of alacrity in calmness and responsiveness in repose that balances the firmness and density that needs to materialize just prior to the impact of the technique.

Cham (沉) – to sink, is the counterpart to fau, focusing on the solidity of the practitioner's mass and concentrated strength of movement at the moment of contact with the opponent. The correlation to sinking relates to a lack of buoyancy stemming from the hardness of full body connectivity. It is a metaphorical manner of meaning solid and unyielding when the technique is manifested. As such, techniques can be viewed as being executed in alternating cycles of soft and hard. The pliancy of the soft stage enables the energy to emanate from coordinated movements; the firmness of the hard phase strengthens the impact force. This balance increases energetic efficiency and optimizes the effectiveness of fighting techniques.

Saam Gung: The Body Mechanics of the Three Bows

In addition to luk ging, the execution of each force relies upon a specific set of motions manipulated by saam gung (三弓) – literally, three bows (as in bow and arrow). The analogy of the bow is used to demonstrate the potential and kinetic energies that are present in the ancient weapon. A drawn bow's energy is in a potential, or yin, state of stored energy; a released arrow represents the bow's kinetic conversion of the yin energy to yang force. Typically, the transitional movements from technique to technique are considered yin while the execution of the actual technique whereby force is issued is regarded as yang. The three bows of the body's trunk are the: dan tian, hung (chest), and bui (back). This trinity addresses the internal principles and external properties of the upper body as intrinsic energy is transformed to martial force within Pak Mei techniques.

The synchronized circulation of internal energy and propulsive bodily behaviors of the upper body stemming from the stance are the sources of tan, tou, fau, and cham. With regard to the dan tian, the return and release of qi to and from this area is physically facilitated by the sinking and rising of the body's core, or abdominal region. The compression of this area physically lowers the qi into the dan tian while its release discharges this intrinsic energy, respectively. This same energy is regulated at the anterior of the upper body by the closing and opening of the chest. As the chest is drawn inward in a closing position, the energy is stored and the qi is withdrawn to the dan tian, assisting the core region in its contracting and sinking action. Conversely, when the chest is in the open position, the energy derived from the stance, directed by the dan tian and its constituents, is released. With regard to the back, the spine needs to maintain an upright alignment while being flexible yet firm – not stiff and solid, to strengthen qi transport and accommodate force-producing activity. The energy of the lower and upper portions of the body are further connected and coordinated through the *ming mun yut* (命門穴; *ming men xue* in Mandarin) – the acupuncture point located below the second lumbar vertebra of the lower back. As this area of the spine expands, it aids the torso's sinking configuration – returning the qi to the dan tian. The middle and upper back supports this structure through the flexing of the latissimus dorsi (muscles of the outer back or lats), which give the back a rounded or curved appearance. Equally, as the ming mun narrows, the rising posture is achieved – transferring the intrinsic energy to the extremities. The transition of the latissimus dorsi to a more flattened or straightened appearance during their release from the flexed position enables the middle and upper back to support the rising movement of the core muscles and opening of the chest.

These upper body behaviors of compression and release (of the dan tian and core region), closing and opening (of the chest cavity), and expansion and narrowing (of the ming mun; flexing and releasing of the latissimus dorsi), respectively, define the process of saam gung.

Within the dynamic of tan, the saam gung work in unison to facilitate a directional force that is actively offensive within a defensive context. The dan tian and core region compresses – or sinks; the thoracic cavity concaves – or closes; and the ming mun expands as the muscles of the back region flex – or curve. In simplified form, the saam gung for this action is a sinking-closing-curving posture.

The uniqueness of tan is that it can act as a complementary and prerequisite directional force for tou as well as provide support for techniques employing simultaneous defensive and offensive maneuvers. As a companion to tou, tan essentially prepares the saam gung to discharge force in an outward direction – opposite to that of tan. The sinking-closing-curving posture sets up the core region, chest cavity, and back muscles to release force in a rising-opening-straightening manner that is indicative of tou. As a result, the compacting and compressing pressures indicative of tan are released and expelled in tou.

The saam gung within the characteristic of fau work collectively to issue force in an angular and ascending direction away from the body. The dan tian and abdominal area releases – or rises; the chest cavity expands – or opens; and the ming mun narrows as the back muscles release – or straighten. In simplified form, the saam gung for this action is a rising-opening-straightening posture. This force is meant to uproot the stability of an opponent's physical foundation as well as rattle that adversary's psychological fortitude.

Unlike the dynamic between tan and tou whereby a symbiotic relationship tends to exist between the two forces, fau does not necessitate cham as a companion force. Fau can function independently given that the prerequisite physiological conditions to emit this force are in place. Given the rising-opening-straightening structure of fau, the prerequisite posture to produce this force would be a sunken-closed-curved body shape indicative of tan. While cham also assumes the saam gung of a sinking-closing-curving position, this is typically the endpoint of the force's journey. Tan on the other hand, customarily serves as the precondition upon which the forces tou and fau exist.

Although the physiology of cham is similar to tan, the directional force emitted is a mirror image to that of tan: cham is outward and downward; tan is inward and downward. The dan tian and core compresses – or sinks; the thoracic cavity concaves – or closes; and the ming mun expands as the back muscles flex – or curve. In simplified form, the saam gung for this action is a sinking-closing-curving posture. To facilitate cham, the practitioner must sink into the Pak Mei stance, anchoring into the ground to secure the integrity of the lower body – one of the primary components in the greater scope of luk ging.

The Combative Implications of Sei Noi Biu Ging

Within the framework of fighting applications, the terms *tan–tou–fau–cham* name the resultant forces that can be produced by the practitioner and exerted upon an opponent. Each energetic dynamic can be combined with another to form complementary combinations within techniques or concentrated into a singular explosive force. For the most part, the names of techniques that are prefaced with the term seung (雙), or double, act in a reinforcing capacity to intensify the strength of an application. As they are being applied, the opponent experiences the distinct combative properties associated with each dynamic force.

Tan and tou maintain the same fighting signatures that were outlined earlier in their figurative definitions. *Tan* assumes the quality of swallowing the opponent's attacks with an inwardly grounding force facilitated by curving body postures and closing movements. The opponent should feel as if he is being consumed by the practitioner's martial methods which leave him exposed and helpless. Ideally in extreme close-quarter stand up encounters, *tan* can be used to unbalance an opponent in order to maximize the impact from the practitioner's striking techniques or against hard surfaces. The devouring action of tan reinforces the practitioner's striking movements by collaboratively disrupting the opponent's balance. As the practitioner sinks, the rooting that occurs fortifies the body's defensive posture and exerts an inward pulling force that ideally unbalances an opponent in a compromisingly downward direction. The turning and rotation that is inherent in Pak Mei methods facilitates repulsive or attractive effects within techniques. When the additional pulling force of tan is factored into the martial equation, the attacking force can be dramatically increased. For example, when a *fung ngaan cheui* (鳳眼搥; phoenix-eye punch) is executed, a pulling force is exerted with the assisting arm while a phoenix-eye punch is carried out with the attacking one. The centripetal rotation of the grab or block in combination with tan essentially pulls the opponent into the phoenix-eye punch. In this case, the inward force of tan amplifies the potency of an executed phoenix-eye strike. As a twofold martial force, *seung jau kiu* (雙抽橋), or double pulling bridges, from the form *Gau Bou Teui* (九步推; 9 Step Push), demonstrates how the swallowing dynamic can generate an advantageous inward momentum that an adversary will find difficult to detect and challenging to counter.

In contrast, *tou* responds to attacks with a refined expulsive force by the lengthening of connective tissues with opening articulations. The effortless yet forceful mechanics fashioned after the purging reflex enables the practitioner to execute techniques fluently, efficiently, and powerfully. The distinguishing feature pertaining to tou is that the martial force propels forward on the horizontal plane. In other words, although the force is initiated at the dan tian and travels upward throughout the torso, it is projected from the body in a direction that is parallel to the ground or on a slight incline. An opponent should be left incapacitated after encountering techniques that seem as if they have been shot from a canon. Within the foundational form *Jik Bou Kyun* (直步拳; Straight Stepping Form), *biu ji* (鏢指; thrusting fingers), is executed in conjunction with a *got kiu* (割橋;

cutting bridge) to bolster the propulsive nature of the technique. As one arm guards against an attack by literally cutting off its intended path, the other actively engages the tou dynamic to simultaneously execute an effective counter. In the form of a pair of reinforcing forces, the energetic effect of *seung taan kiu* (雙彈橋; double flicking bridges), from the pillar routine, *Sap Baat Mo Kiu* (十八摩橋; 18 Stripping Bridges), originates in the stance, is processed through the trunk, and projected outward from the arms and hands. To ensure the effectiveness of this force, all strikes target vital areas that are at the practitioner's chest and neck level instead of the opponent's. For example, against a taller adversary, the practitioner may attack the opponent's diaphragm or rib cage rather than reach for the chest, clavicles or throat leaving the practitioner's own vital zones exposed.

As a fighting force, the goals of *fau* are to uproot, disorient, and disable an opponent, thereby preventing him from being able to attack effectively. The floating model inspires the practitioner to execute techniques in an upward direction similar to a submerged ball speeding toward the water's surface after being released. Through lengthening postures and opening movements, the integrated force is launched like a rocket, rising and ready to explode upon impact. This applied force is actually known as *sing ging* (升勁), or rising force. The opponent should experience the sensation of being unable to secure a firm foundation as if he were floating on a body of water. This enables the practitioner to exercise greater control over the opponent's distressed movements. A highly developed ability to issue fau is found in the technique *ba wong ging jau* (霸王敬酒), or tyrannical king offers wine. In this technique, the advanced practitioner is able to apply fau to strengthen an upward striking throat grab with the right hand while being assisted by the other with *lit sau* (捩手; tearing hand). In extremely close situations where there is still room for effective striking, the stealthy thrust of *yam yeung seung cheui* (陰陽雙搥), or yin and yang double strike, from the system's highest set *Maang Fu Cheut Lam* (猛虎出林; Fierce Tiger Comes Out of the Forest), exemplifies the upward and uprooting nature of *fau*.

In combat, cham is applied as a suppressing force that pressures, exhausts and ultimately overwhelms an opponent. The concept of sinking is manifested as a downward strength, refined by rounded body postures and closing actions, and strengthened by the sheer force of gravity. The practitioner's techniques should be as solid and weighted as stones being plunged into the ocean. In turn, the opponent must withstand the feeling of drowning under a relentless wave of counter-maneuvers and offensive tactics. The technique *kap jeung* (扱掌; extracting palm), simultaneously implementing a suppressing palm attack with an inward pull facilitated by a left grab, exemplifies the effectiveness of complementary force dynamics. Striking techniques making use of *cham* are typically direct and aimed at the abdominal cavity, groin, or *kwa* – the inguinal ligament. *Seung jong cheui* (雙撞搥) or double strikes, from the routine Eagle Claw Sticking Bridge (鷹爪黏橋) better known as *Ying Jaau Nim Kiu*, demonstrates the powerful and straightforward striking methods that were adapted from the Dragon Shape Kung Fu system (龍形拳術). When the practitioner's footwork and structural alignment are in place, the downward force can lead to locks, throws, or takedowns that can be applied to any of the opponent's body parts. Ideally, a singular movement involving cham can incapacitate a person. A chained series of suppressing forces – simultaneous subduing and striking, however, is intended to annihilate him.

Over time, the experienced Pak Mei practitioner understands which combination of forces to apply for optimum effectiveness during the uniqueness of each situation.

Baat Ging: The Eight Manifestations of Ging

Baat ging (八勁) refers to the 8 primary manifestations of force that can be executed in Pak Mei techniques. When luk ging and sei noi biu ging are proficiently performed, the ability to produce force and give it direction is established. The issuing force can assume 8 mannerisms – meaning how this force will be used within the framework of a technique. Each characteristic conveys a unique way in which the force can be utilized. Typically, multiple manifestations of baat ging concurrently occur during the execution of a single Pak Mei technique. Regardless of whether the forces are the same or different, they always assist each other in a reinforcing manner.

All techniques have two components or stages: yin and yang. Techniques are considered yin en route to a target and yang upon execution or impact. The flexible and limber phase of a technique conserves muscular exertion and prevents tension and stiffness from hampering the efficient circulation of qi to the intended areas where force will be issued. This period of yin is essential to effectively employing baat ging. The optimal release of force, the yang phase, is dependent upon: fluid qi flow, proper structure and mechanics, and martial physics – all facilitated by the yin phase of the technique. The eight forces require a harmonious balance of yin and yang phases to successfully execute a technique.

Bin

Bin (鞭) means to whip. In order to appropriately emulate this force, the practitioner must have a mastery of the performance of relaxed and firm movements. The elasticity during the yin phase enables ging to pass through the extremities smoothly; the force is then released upon the moment of impact, or the yang stage. Typically, bin is a striking or breaking technique that travels outward from the body. Additionally, it characteristically travels across the width of the body before discharging the force into its intended target. Novice and intermediate practitioners may initially overemphasize or exaggerate this particular movement; however, these gross motor exaggerations eventually evolve toward more refined and compact maneuvers during advanced stages of practice. An example of bin is found in the technique gwa cheui (掛槌), or hanging strike.

Got

Got (割) means to cut. This action makes reference to two connotations associated with cutting: to cut-off as in to prevent or stop from entering or to sever the incoming attack from its initiator. Got utilizes an inward pulling force to either block or actively attack. Within this context, the motion is typically to the side of the body. In collaboration with the other hand, got has the ability to change into a breaking or dislocation technique. The range of motion required to execute this particular ging is relatively small compared to the requirements of the other forces; however, due to the subtleties of the movement and the limitation of spatial range, the finer details of torsion – twisting and turning motions, need to be practiced to perfection. On an elementary level, got can function effectively as a block. In advanced levels, got assumes a more aggressive and destructive nature. An elementary example of got is found in the blocking aspect of *fung ngaan cheui* (鳳眼槌), or phoenix-eye punch.

Waan

Waan (挽) means to pull, particularly in the manner of an inward arc. This hooking motion traverses the front of the body, sweeping attacks in a direction that compromises the opponent's stability. This provides the practitioner with the opportunity to penetrate the opponent's vital areas that have been exposed as a result of a well-executed technique incorporating this particular force. Waan is one of the most sophisticated of the eight ging as it requires a mastery of timing, range, proper mechanics, sensitivity, and gumption. These attributes are more products of a practitioner's experience, intuition and intelligence rather than the sheer inherent effectiveness of a technique. An example of waan is found in one of the most advanced techniques found in the Pak Mei Kung Fu system: *waan sau fu jaau* (挽手虎爪), or pulling hand tiger claw. The highest degree of aggressiveness and the greatest level of seizing and tearing skills are required to correctly apply this technique.

Jong

Jong (撞) means to collide or bump against. Within Pak Mei Kung Fu, jong refers to a ramming force. This ging characteristically discharges from the front of the body since the body's weight ideally supports the strength of the force from this reinforcing position. The leverage afforded by this supportive structure enables the ramming force of jong ging to be applied optimally. The greater part of the practitioner's energy and force is channeled into the technique employing this ging as it converts from yin to yang. Due to the colliding nature of this particular force, jong is typically used as a strike to breach the barriers protecting an opponent's vital organs, to fracture limbs, or to act as an overwhelming counteroffensive. The technique that best illustrates this force, *jong kiu* (撞橋) – colliding bridge, is found in Pak Mei's signature form Gau Bou Teui.

Chung

Chung (衝) means to rush against. In a martial context, chung refers to an outward charging force that is quite similar to jong ging. It is generally released from the front of the body, using the practitioner's firm foundation to support this particular force behind a technique.

Chung ging is considered one of the more fundamental ging within the classification of eight forces. Due its straightforward characteristic, chung can be used rather quickly and comfortably by beginner level practitioners. One of the key factors determining the effectiveness of chung ging is a practitioner's range with respect to reach. Its maximum force peaks within a practitioner's close yet uncompromising range. If the technique is too close it will be hampered; if it is overextended it will leave the practitioner exposed. The first opportunity that a practitioner has to experience this force is through the technique *chung cheui* (衝槌), or charging punch. It is similar to an uppercut in Western boxing; however, the force guides the technique up the practitioner's centerline and discharges it in an upward and outward manner.

Taan

Taan (彈) means to flick or bounce. This force is similar to bin ging, or whipping force; however, the range of taan takes place within the parameters of the sides of the body. The motions incorporating this ging typically travel in an outward direction to the sides of the body. While bin's whipping force requires elasticity, torsion, and a slight wind-up to emit the force, the compacted force of taan ging requires an even greater level of elasticity, a more refined sense of torsion, and little to no wind-up prior to issuing the force. As a result, reliance upon outstanding body mechanics and unobstructed and reinforcing qi flow is essential to the effectiveness of this ging. The primary use of this ging is to penetrate sensitive areas and to strike vital points on an opponent's body. A Pak Mei practitioner's first experience with taan ging is through the technique *hat yi lou mai* (乞倚勞米), or beggar asking for rice – the first movement following the Pak Mei salute in *Jik Bou Kyun* (直步拳).

Sok

Sok (索) literally means rope. Within Pak Mei Kung Fu, sok alludes to a yanking or sudden jerking motion, as if one were gripping and applying vigorous tugs on a thick rope. This is typically an inward action applied toward the side of the body. Seizing techniques within Pak Mei characteristically employ sok ging to disrupt an opponent's balance and direct the individual toward a compromising position. Novice practitioners will tend to rely on muscular strength when applying this force while advanced practitioners will draw upon the coordination of luk ging and saam gung to execute this force. It is important to note that this was great master Cheung Lai Chuen's favorite ging to perform. He found it so essential that he incorporated this ging as the closing movement prior to each form's closing salute within his assemblage of imported forms. The technique that best represents this force is *sok ging* (索勁), or yanking force.

Pun

Pun (盤) is defined as a tray or plate. Its martial connotation refers to a coiling motion, particularly a circular infiltrating action. The distinctive trademark of pun is that it maneuvers around the perimeter of an attack and penetrates a vital point on the opponent's body. It generally exercises an outward motion encircling and deflecting an incoming attack. Similar to waan ging, pun ging requires the same mastery of timing, range, proper mechanics, sensitivity, and gumption. However, precision and accuracy are additional prerequisites that are needed to properly execute this force. Perhaps one of the most advanced gings within this set of eight force mannerisms, pun ging relies upon the finesse and subtlety of a practitioner's movements within a technique as this specific ging guides it. An example of pun is found in the striking aspect of *fung ngaan cheui* – phoenix-eye punch, whereas the strike spirals toward its target. Aside from supporting the issuing of ging, the twining motion can effectively maneuver around an incoming strike and offensively defend the practitioner by both deflecting and penetrating through the opponent's attack.

The blueprint for martial power as it has been presented in this section provides a practitioner with the guidance to refine one's issuing force to maximize Pak Mei techniques. However, practice and progress should be aligned with the individual's personal physicality, aptitude, and age. As a practitioner matures, it is hopeful that the individual's natural attributes are optimized and challenging areas are minimized.

While ging is a significant facet of the body methods and physical movements in Pak Mei Kung Fu, a further collection of cultural concepts, martial principles, and training procedures contribute to the completeness of the system.

CHAPTER TWO

Philosophy & Theory

"Theory helps us to bear our ignorance of facts."

- George Santayana,

Philosopher and poet (1863 – 1952)

Taoism within Pak Mei Kung Fu

Taoism is considered one of the three primary schools of Chinese thought alongside Buddhism and Confucianism, contributing to the basis of traditional Chinese culture. In general, Taoism has been known to exist in the form of philosophical, religious, medical, alchemical, and martial manifestations. The most recognized figure and text associated with Taoism is *Lao Zi* and the *Dao De Jing* (老子, 道德經 – The Classic of the Way and Its Virtue), respectively.

The term Tao, or Dao (道), in Chinese literally translates to road or way. Within the philosophical framework of Taoism, the Tao refers to *the way* of nature. For the individual, the Tao is the way of the experience of the process and destiny of life. It is spiritual, but non-religious through the introspection and awareness of oneself and nature. The fundamental emphasis of Taoism is that non-action will give rise to the ideal action. In other words, if individuals let situations run their own course, and officials govern by doing nothing, then as a collective, the universe will be in harmony. In essence, everything has its role in this world as we know it. And, for harmony and order to be maintained, everything must carry out its role as it was intended by nature and the universe. To go against nature is to go against the Tao, which will produce disharmony, chaos, and ruin. In theory, Taoism is ideal. In reality, the flaws found in Taoism are apparent and countless. However, an extensive examination of Taoism is beyond the scope of this work.

Within the framework of Chinese martial arts, Taoism provides martial methods with a sense of martial philosophy and strategy by encouraging a practitioner to follow the Tao, or the way, and to acknowledge and understand the interplay of yin and yang, in order to achieve universal harmony.

Yin and Yang: The Ultimate Expression

The concept of yin and yang is deeply embedded within Chinese culture. Its implications are so vast that it can be used to define the various dualities in nature or even to expound the creation of the universe. In simplest terms, *yin* (陰; *yam* in Cantonese) is considered a phase of inactivity that is associated with darkness, passiveness, winter, night, and the female while *yang* (陽; *yeung* in

Cantonese) is viewed as a state of activity that is respectively related to light, activeness, summer, daytime, and the male. As a pair of opposing phases interacting in cycles of dominance and recession, neither yin nor yang is completely removed from the other. When a condition reaches its apex, it will transition to its opposite phase: night gives way to day; winter evolves to summer; the tide recedes and rolls in. The yin or yang state is not a fixed attribute, but rather a cyclical phase, assuming either quality depending on its capacity with regard to other factors. In other words, the potential for something to be either yin or yang depends upon the situation to determine its characteristic. It is this simultaneous display of simplicity and sophistication by way of the concept of yin and yang (陰陽) that revolutionized Pak Mei Kung Fu.

With regard to structure and movement, yin and yang can be used to identify the passive and active areas throughout the body that contribute to a sense of systemic stability. In accordance with the properties of yin and yang, any portion of the body in a state of emptiness, regression, or gathering is considered yin while the areas experiencing amplitude, ascendency, or dispersion are yang. During training, the practitioner is able to keenly observe the bodily behaviors that produce this balance. For example, the leg that bears weight within a posture is considered yang while the one that is in a phase of return or readiness is deemed yin. In the case of the Pak Mei stance, although the practitioner's balance is evenly distributed between both lower limbs, it is important not to weight both legs as this will compromise one's mobility. An understanding of yin and yang within this context enables the practitioner to step effectively and root firmly during the execution of techniques in both practice and application.

Pak Mei techniques will use the duality of yin and yang to describe the directionality of its *sau faat* (手法; hand methods). The arrangement of the palm typically determines the characteristic that the hands will assume. In general, an inward facing palm is usually considered yin, a defensive mode, and an outward facing one is considered yang, an attacking phase. On a fundamental level, the technique *gang sau* (耕手; tilling hands) is considered a yin phase since the palm of this technique faces inward, defensively sweeping away an unforeseen attack. Conversely, *seung teui jeung* (雙推掌; double pushing palms) is an actively offensive maneuver that is yang with the palms directed outward. Another manner of movement employing yin and yang is *jyun* (轉), or turning, more appropriately acknowledged as torsion – the inherent rotational and twining forces within Pak Mei techniques. This subtle yet refined action is a signature motion that defines the principle of *mo* (摩) – to grind or strip, in Pak Mei Kung Fu. This twining force acts defensively to disrupt seizing attempts by an opponent and offensively to strengthen the force of an attack. An unexpected wrist grab from an assailant can be broken by an upward yin arm rotation followed by a counter-twisting and tearing yang *fu jaau* (虎爪; tiger claw). This technique is collectively known as *chyun mo sau* (穿摩手; piercing stripping hands) from Gau Bou Teui. In a different scenario, what was typically an upward yin arm becomes an actively yang arm-dislocation or break on the opponent, and the twining fu jaau can respond in a yin manner as it sinks to deflect a sudden mid-section attack.

The exigencies of distinct situations will determine the yin or yang qualities of techniques.

As it pertains to positioning, the properties of yin and yang convey the nature of sections of the body throughout movements as well as inform the practitioner of one's spatial advantages and weaknesses against an opponent. Yin and yang are continuously exhibited in the arms and legs, and between the upper and lower parts of the body. Within postures, the extended arm and retracted hand exhibits a state of balanced surveillance – neither imposing nor cowering. Should the forward arm be actively yang, the hind hand should be defensively yin. Conversely, if the rear hand is in a yang phase, the lead arm should be in a supportive yin stage ready to transition to an offensive yang trait. There are occasions when both extremities of the upper body may be actively yang or a countering yin. When this occurs, the lower limbs will assume a phase that will equalize the upper body actions. For example, as both arms execute the yang-based *seung teui jeung* (double pushing palms), the stance will be engaged in a complementary yin-dominant mode. On the other hand, should both arms become entangled in a comprehensive guard that is inherently yin, the legs should apply a yang-influenced *gwai ma* (跪馬; kneeling stance) to regain the tactical advantage by furtively attacking the adversary's foundation. As one maneuvers to gain an advantageous position against an opponent, the yin and yang model reveals the type of tactics that are specific to certain maneuvers. The pressuring step, *bik bou* (逼步), enables the practitioner to enter and occupy an opponent's personal space in a very yang-dominant fashion. This allows the practitioner to create a pressure-sensitive setting that provides another distraction and obstacle for the opponent to overcome. However, to disengage and evade an overwhelming attack, *teui ma* (退馬; retreating stance) assists the practitioner in withdrawing to a safe zone. While this yin-mannered movement is a defensive maneuver, it can also adopt a yang state of activity by luring an opponent into a compromising position as in the technique *teui bou mo kiu* (退步摩橋; retreating step, stripping bridge) from the routine *Ying Jaau Nim Kiu*. Here, the receding movement takes away the energy of the full brunt of an opponent's attack which creates a state of oppositional yin. This allows the practitioner to optimally attack the opponent who is in a failed post-attack phase and must quickly regain his balance and composure to successfully follow up with a counter tactic.

In terms of fighting strategy, the Pak Mei practitioner's attitude toward combat is outlined in two particular verses:

1) *Nei bat loi; ngo bat faat* (你不來; 我不發): You don't come; I won't start

2) *Bat yung maan lik* (不用蠻力): Do not use brute strength

The first statement defines the art as a system of self-defense; the second is a description of how techniques must be executed should the need arise for them to be used. When provocative behavior escalates to physical violence, the aggressor who launches the first blow is technically at fault. Particularly in today's litigious society, such aggravated and even accidental actions carry severe penalties in the court of law. As a

46

result, responding to, rather than initiating an assault enables the practitioner to be perceived as an individual acting in self-defense. On a tactical level, the Pak Mei practitioner seeks to exploit the opponent's weaknesses during the yin phase – the period immediately following the peak of an adversary's attack. This enables the practitioner to steal the opponent's stability and to counter in a less detectable manner. As confrontational distances decrease, greater technical and sensing abilities that support straightforward and intrepid techniques are indispensable over less refined and riskier martial methods. Since the opponent is in a compromised position, there is no need to use brute strength – a less efficient form of martial power and efficacy.

The yin and yang dynamic is ubiquitously present in all aspects of natural phenomena, social interaction, and personal activity. Understanding the principles of yin and yang enables one to face the spontaneities of life encounters in a more manageable and less confounded manner. Within Pak Mei Kung Fu, this Taoist concept allows one to optimize the outcomes of both commonplace situations as well as extraordinary circumstances.

Breathing Methodologies

The manner in which the breath is controlled can greatly increase one's martial power or significantly curb its potency. Regulating the breath leads to normalizing the body's physiology, thereby maximizing the flow of qi throughout the system.

In martial practice, the two primary types of breathing are based upon Buddhist and Taoist approaches.

There are merits and concerns to both approaches.

Qi and Qigong

Qi (氣; *hei* in Cantonese) is a concept that is the foundation of Traditional Chinese Medicine and an essential complement to Asian martial arts.

Documented and detailed in China's ancient medical text, *Huangdi Neijing* (黃帝內經; The Yellow Emperor's Inner Classic), circa 1st Century BCE, qi is a term that has been referred to in modern times as simply as air or breath in its literal form and acknowledged as life force or vital energy within a more comprehensive classification. The character 氣 represents steam rising from cooking rice, and like the steam, qi within the body is colorless, formless, and weightless. Its actuality can be experienced through sensations such as heat, tingling, or firmness throughout the body.

On a basic level, qi is said to originate from the kidneys. It is then transferred to the dan tian to be stored and transported throughout the various parts of the body via *jing luo* (經絡), or meridians. Through unobstructed pathways, qi will optimally energize the internal organs and strengthen the body as a whole. On the other hand, meridians that are blocked can prevent bodily functions from performing at full capacity which can lead to illness and disease. These channels should be opened by way of the dan tian so that there is a central point of coordination and base for qi circulation.

An expanded explanation of qi divides the concept into two foundational composite classifications: prenatal and postnatal. *Yuan qi* (元氣; *yun hei*) – literally original qi, refers to the inherited energy and intelligence that has been transmitted by the genetic coding of one's biological parents. It is the qi that one has acquired from birth. In combination with one's *jing* (精), or essence, this prenatal qi is stored in the kidneys. Postnatal qi is the vital essence that is produced throughout one's lifetime as a result of the air that one breathes, the quality of food that is consumed, and the amount of time and effort dedicated to the actual cultivation of qi. This qi acquired after birth is composed of 3 primary subcategories: *kong qi* (空氣; *hung hei*), *gu qi* (穀氣; *guk hei*), and *zong qi* (宗氣; *jung hei*). Kong qi – literally air qi, is the energy derived from the intake of oxygen, and gu qi, or grain qi, is the result of the types of food that one eats. Zong qi, better known as gathering qi, is the combination of kong qi and gu qi. When zong qi is assisted by yuan qi, the former is converted to *zheng qi* (正氣; *jing hei*), or proper qi. There are two characteristics to zheng qi: a yin nature called *ying qi* (營氣; *ying hei*), or nourishing energy, which is transported through the meridians, and a yang state known as *wei qi* (衛氣; *wai hei*), a defensive energy that guards the individual against invasive pathogens. Collectively, this process defines qi production within the human body.

Qigong (氣功; *hei gung*), literally steam achievement, refers to the methods by which qi is cultivated. In Chinese culture, qigong is practiced across a broad range of disciplines that includes, but is not limited to: medical, health, spiritual, martial, and folk arts. Within Chinese martial arts, one of the more influential methods of qigong is the *Yijin Jing* (易筋經; *Yik Gan Ging*), better known as The Muscle/Tendon Change Classic which was purportedly created during the 6th Century CE by Bodhidharma (菩提達摩; *Putidamo/Pou Tai Daat Mo*), the Buddhist monk recognized as the patriarch of *Chan* Buddhism (禪; *sim*) in China. Due to his affiliation with the Shaolin Temple (少林寺), considered the folkloric fountainhead of Chinese martial arts, this classic method was adapted by many martial artists and their respective clans to enhance their overall training.

Currently, there are countless forms of qigong that cater to a variety of objectives. Within Pak Mei Kung Fu, qigong methods are exercised as static postures, within dynamic movement, and throughout combative techniques. While specific movements are trained, a particular breathing methodology is linked to those actions in order to sustain one's stamina and maximize one's martial power. These inherent breathing patterns have typically been incorporated from two distinct qigong traditions: one Buddhist, and the other, Taoist.

Water and Fire: Regulating the Qi

Prior to embarking upon an exploration of Buddhist and Taoist qigong, the concept of water and fire must be explained. *Kan* (坎: *ham*; to snare or capture) is the trigram of the *ba gua* (八卦; *baat gwa* – the eight Taoist divining symbols) that represents water; *li* (離: *lei*; to leave or separate) is the trigram representing fire. The terms *shui* (水; *seui*) and *huo* (火; *fo*), typically used for water and fire, are also commonly used to indicate the concept of water and fire in this context. The metaphysical water-fire relationship is the dynamic that regulates qi activity within the body. This interplay is associated with yin and yang, but these facets themselves are not yin and yang. The water-fire relationship is the source and process for reaching yin and yang harmony within the body.

In Traditional Chinese Medicine, the belief is that balance is maintained in the body when a harmonious relationship exists between water and fire. The kidneys are associated with the water element while the heart is affiliated with the fire element. Hence, Kidney-Water cools and nourishes Heart-Fire, and Heart-Fire warms Kidney-Water. This continuous interaction is known as the mutual production cycle of Water and Fire. As such, water is aligned with yin, and fire is connected with yang. When there is an overabundance of either component, an imbalance occurs.

The water-fire relationship as it pertains to martial qigong is as follows: Buddhist qigong promotes water qi; Taoist qigong elevates fire qi. Each method yields an outcome that is relative to the practitioner's goals, either raising levels of water qi or increasing amounts of fire qi. In either case, balance needs to be achieved.

The Buddhist Method: Conventional Abdominal Breathing

Buddhist qigong typically focused on spiritual development and the attainment of enlightenment. Practitioners of Buddhist qigong characteristically remained faithful to the original aims of the tradition and opposed any nuances that would supposedly enhance its practice outside of its framework. In this sense, reservation served to preserve the practice essentially in its purest form.

Deep breathing methods employed in Buddhist qigong travel down to the dan tian area. When one breathes using the Buddhist method, the abdominal region expands during the inhalation and contracts during the exhalation. This conventional abdominal breathing is similar to the type of breathing that is used on a daily basis. Most breathing is typically limited to the thoracic cavity or chest area, but the abdominal region still expands on the intake and contracts on the release. This familiar action is both comfortable and calming. Ideally, it increases relaxation and activates the parasympathetic nervous system – a division of the autonomic nervous system that stimulates rest and assuagement. The internal massage produced by the stomach muscles used to facilitate the deep abdominal breathing serves to energize the viscera and strengthen qi flow. Additionally, as the air intake is increased, blood cells are oxygenated, enhancing the richness of the circulation and improving a sense of mindfulness and clarity.

In the metaphysical sense, Buddhist qigong serves to cool the fire qi that makes the body too yang. The general theory passed down from ancient texts and apprenticeship is that the body is typically in a yang state – a yin state occurs when one experiences physical maladies or general health illnesses. When the body is in a constant state of yang, it becomes too hot, leading to cellular degeneration which exacerbates aging and illness. The water qi furnished by the Buddhist breathing method neutralizes the abundance of fire qi in the body and essentially cools it down. This in turn acts as an anti-aging agent – promoting global balance in the body which leads to longevity.

The Taoist Method: Reverse Abdominal Breathing

Taoist qigong is generally employed in the quest for longevity or to enhance martial performance. Taoists were much more open to experimentation with qigong than Buddhists were. As a result, many obscure and even peculiar manners of practice were adopted into Taoist conventions. Of particular interest to this text is the incorporation of Taoist breathing into martial techniques.

While the Taoist method also utilizes deep abdominal breathing, the abdominal action is opposite that of the Buddhist technique – the abdominal region contracts during the inhalation and expands during the exhalation. This reverse breathing method increases the efficiency of channeling qi to the extremities and other body parts that can benefit martially from the Taoist process. Keen Taoist observations and the implementation of praxis from esoteric principles have led to further advancements in power production and the emission of force, particularly with regard to the incorporation of breathing patterns infused within martial techniques.

Within a metaphysical framework, Taoist qigong employs fire qi to stimulate hormone productivity while raising the body's ability to emit force optimally. Fire qi that is associated with the heart warms the water qi of the kidneys. The profusion of fire qi stimulates hormone production, and of particular interest, testosterone – the male hormone accountable for producing and maintaining male secondary sex characteristics. Within the realm of testosterone, aggression is typically elevated when the production of the hormone is increased. This aggressive nature has characteristically been infused in the manner in which Pak Mei techniques are executed, but not in the conduct or behavior of the practitioner. While the coordination of luk ging facilitates the structure and mechanics of emitting martial force, the Taoist breathing method reinforces Pak Mei techniques by leading the qi to the extremities.

In the highest and ideal levels of practice, qi is led to the ends of the extremities and can be effectively emitted without physical contact. This is the foundation for qigong healing.

The Realities of Each Qigong Method

Preferences for either Buddhist or Taoist breathing methods are entirely dependent upon the teacher. The reasons for an instructor's partiality can range from sheer unawareness to a belief in the ultimate safeguarding of the *secrets* of the system.

Buddhist qigong has been emphasized for a number of sound reasons. First and foremost, with the onset of modern warfare with modern weapons, the need for intense physical training to such a demanding degree has diminished. In times of village raids by bandits or actual battlefield clashes, martial skills needed to be trained to the highest degree for sheer survival. Additionally, training methods and specialized skills were kept secret to maintain an element of surprise against opponents, depriving them of the opportunity to identify and devise strategies to counter such methods. In modern situations, sophisticated self-defense methods using fundamental physics, physiology, psychology and common street smarts are enough to avoid or escape violent situations. Intense training in the present sense has been reserved more for those involved in modern martial sports or the military – in either case, each area has had the luxury of sports science or a specific set of scientific approaches to enhance training and prevent injury over the trial and error experiments of past traditional Chinese practitioners.

With regard to the teacher, very few individuals received such meticulous and detailed training from the great master, Cheung Lai Chuen. Those in the local militia or military generally learned fundamental fighting skills in a large group setting; those in village locations or one of the satellite schools under Cheung Lai Chuen's banner may have been taught modified versions of authentic techniques; those close to Cheung Lai Chuen may have learned authentic techniques without substantiating principles or appropriate applications; the handful, literally, closest to Cheung Lai Chuen were privileged to the knowledge of the variations and primary principles of Pak Mei Kung Fu. For these reasons, general Pak Mei practitioners who chose to teach the martial material that they learned were somewhat limited in what they could convey in terms of Pak Mei principles and qigong theory since they were not privileged to such instruction. On the other hand, indoor disciples valued their transmissions from the great master to such a degree that they typically withheld such important information as a means to gain an upper hand on their students or simply made the decision not to teach at all. As a result, breathing principles were essentially based upon the most natural method, or Buddhist approach, since many failed to learn or chose to withhold the Taoist procedure.

In reference to one's global health, Buddhist qigong is the safest route physically and mentally, and most efficient spiritual practice toward gaining self-awareness and attaining enlightenment. The water qi that is cultivated serves to balance the fire qi that must be kept in check. A surplus of fire qi without safety measures to ensure the equilibrium between water and fire will lead to both physical and mental instabilities. On the physical level, this will lead to premature aging and degeneration of the organs. On the mental level, an overly heated body agitates the mind, which can lead to memory loss, anxiety, irrational behavior, and psychosis.

With the constant bombardment of stressors on a daily basis ranging from financial fears to family affairs and peer politics to romantic matters, the Buddhist method helps to sort out those issues by relaxing the body and calming the mind, eliciting mindfulness and inducing lucid thoughts.

The Taoist method of qi circulation and energy manipulation has traditionally been the most promoted approach within Pak Mei Kung Fu. Whether the internal concepts were imported from other martial clans by savvy practitioners, learned from open-minded seniors well-versed in Pak Mei and willing to share such classified material, or directly imparted from Cheung Lai Chuen, Taoist breathing strategies have typically served the martially-minded population of Pak Mei practitioners. This particular method of breathing infused within Pak Mei techniques increases force-issuing efficiency, facilitates the development of defensive armor through the ribs conditioning activity of *dip gwat gung* (疊骨功; folding bones achievement), and supports the aggressive and relentless mindset in executing Pak Mei techniques.

With such extreme training and conditioning, both physiological and psychological hazards are to be expected; furthermore, methods used to temper the overabundance of fire qi need to be implemented so that the practitioner does not succumb to the adverse effects of intense training that has incorporated Taoist qigong methodologies. Safeguards are found in both the training environment and a keen sense of awareness. In traditional training halls, whenever the Chinese character for fire, 火, appears on an altar, a plaque, or within poetic couplets, it is typically represented upside down. One particular purpose of inverting this character is to serve as a constant reminder for the practitioner to keep in check increased levels of fire qi.

When the body grows metaphysically too hot, an individual's judgment can become clouded, the ability to make rational decisions may be forfeited, and in severe cases psychosis can result from the rising levels of hormonal toxicity accumulated from incorrect practice or improper guidance. Under these circumstances, levels of aggression can lead to anger which can escalate to violence. As such, an unstable mind coupled with hostile behavior will yield disastrous and even fatal results. When a practitioner senses changes in temper or experiences tendencies toward an unproductive emotional direction, countermeasures need to be put into practice. One of the most direct methods to offset the potential for global instability is to complement the inherent Taoist qigong with water qi enhancing qigong. Within Pak Mei Kung Fu, this equalizing effect can come in quite a few forms that include: *jaam jong hei gung* (站樁氣功, standing post breath work), *cho gung* (坐功, sitting meditation), and *maan kyun* (慢拳, slow boxing method). All of these approaches are based in Buddhist qigong practices that stimulate water qi production to cool the fire qi that is capable of degenerating the body and mind.

The source of safe, efficient and effective practice is to understand and implement a standard of balance. Excessive fire qi can promote long-term damaging effects to both the body and the mind; excessive water qi can lead to illumination and clarity, but hamper force production with regard to martial power. Depending on the priority of the teacher and the needs of the individual, a Buddhist or Taoist qigong method may be emphasized. Ultimately, it will be the individual practitioner who will have to come to terms with equalizing the water-fire relationship within the body's qi dynamic for optimum health as well as maximized martial efficiency.

Intent in Internalization and Combat

In Chinese martial arts, yi (意) is the actively intelligent mind that must initially lead qi to the areas where the visceral organs will be energized and ging will be expressed. When this conscious connection develops into instinctive proactivity, the qi will flow efficiently, effectively, and naturally, strengthening the muscles and surrounding tissue so that the body will be comprehensively optimized. Once sheer muscular strength is no longer necessary, qi no longer needs to be willfully led by yi, and maximized martial power is issued from an integrated body, ging is realized.

A focused yi, freely flowing qi, and fully aligned body illustrates the fundamental characteristics of the internal process of a martial art. Should the yi be unsettled, the qi will proceed haphazardly, leading the body to experience a systemic imbalance. Conversely, should the body be misaligned, the qi will not be able to appositely access every area of the body, ultimately affecting the quality of yi facilitation. Therefore, it is of vital importance to establish this connection at the onset of one's introduction into the system.

During the early stages of solo practice and throughout one's lifetime of refinement, the relationship between intent and movement is trained and maintained by adhering to a formula of five key terms: *wai* (為), *yin* (演), *yuk* (勗), *san* (伸), and *lin* (連) – envision, execute, enliven, extend, and ensue, respectively. Wai, literally to serve as, instructs the practitioner to move with the mind's eye. In other words, one must perform physical actions in a manner that recreates the actual applications for those movements. For example, as the technique *chyun sam fung ngaan cheui* (穿心鳳眼搥; piercing the heart phoenix-eye punch) is exhibited in solo practice, one should genuinely visualize the action penetrating through the opponent's defenses and targeting the vital organ. Yin, to perform, requires that one moves with the correct alignment and structure, engaging the appropriate body parts throughout each and every movement. The mind actively monitors this to ensure that the individual's martial power will be properly placed during applications. Yuk, to stimulate, informs the practitioner to train in a lively rather lifeless manner. Inattentiveness and sluggish behaviors will hamper one's energy level and spirit, while a focused nature and dynamic action will raise one's overall presence. San, literally to extend, refers to the full extension of movements to refine one's penetration power. The complete extension and follow-through of movements during solo practice is critical in training the body to fully release the force that drives techniques. Partially completed movements, particularly at the joints, will check the maximum potential of power that can be exerted within techniques. While this commitment is risky and dangerous in actual combat since exposed joints can be manipulated, it is essential during practice to open all points of articulation so that the qi can travel freely to energize the extremities. Finally, lin, to be continuous, advises the practitioner to be uninterrupted and steady during both practice and in physical altercations. One needs to move in an unwavering manner from start to finish – unshaken in focus and unbroken in action. This serves to fortify one's fortitude and to promote the continuity of techniques.

In combat, intent refers to the commitment to engage in an altercation. This martial spirit is captured in the Pak Mei maxim: *cheut sau bat lau ching; lau ching bat cheut sau* (出手不留情, 留情不出手) – Should your hands have to go out, do not hold back your feelings or intent; if you hold back your intent, do not put out your hands.

Displays of intent are, in reality, representations of individual personalities and stages of development. One's manifestation of yi should be balanced in accordance with the properties of yin and yang. The eyes should be alert; the mind should be calm; and, the body must be poised. This is the optimal state of expressive intent, or yi. In this phase, the practitioner is internally dynamic and externally explosively with techniques, should the absolute need arise for them to be employed.

In one's youth, it is quite natural to overly express one's fire with fierce eyes and a harsh countenance. In some cases it is merely meant to intimidate the opponent; in others, it is intended to summon one's killing intent, or saat hei. While the intent appears overtly in the former instance, it may actually be exhibited with reservation. In the latter mode, the outer expression is characteristically fueled by an internal combination of adrenaline, elevated levels of testosterone, and a crude temperament which in the long term can lead to paranoia and eventual psychosis due to the disproportionate degree of fire qi that is disbursed to support this state. Psychologically against a skilled opponent, this expressive appearance could cause an adversary to raise his guard and intensify his own attacks.

On the other hand, a dull set of eyes and meek expression conveys a lack of gumption, whether the case may actually be true or not. The mind may be unsure and the combative intent absent, negatively impacting one's ability to execute techniques effectively. Although this yin appearance can be used to mislead an opponent into underestimating one's skill, it is an outward expression that can compromise one's overall martial spirit and fuel an opponent's offensive against an individual's apparent weakness.

A refined yi establishes the internal integrity and martial spirit that defines a quality martial art. It needs to be carefully cultivated and mindfully monitored to be maintained.

Fongsung: The Skill of Tension Release

The concept of *fongsung* (放鬆; loosen/relax) refers to an essential martial quality that facilitates efficient and effective movement. When the practitioner's structure is sound, body methods are efficient, and intent is applicable, the body needs to be in a state of relaxed readiness to establish a productive delivery system. In any activity, muscular tension and tightness of the joints are obstructions that prevent maximized movement and mobility from materializing. As a result, premature fatigue and an inability to ideally complete physical actions can occur.

When the body is lithe and limber, it responds productively and reacts in a livelier manner. Less effort is required to accomplish what can be considered strenuous tasks. More importantly, there is a reduced reliance upon muscular might which is a principal cause of tension and stiffness when the body solely engages this form of strength. This tension-free state, however, must not be mistaken with a limp and aimless expression. Excessively slack and lifeless movements lack the solidity and firmness to deeply penetrate targets. Effective techniques rely upon a balance between a relaxed delivery and a dense impact.

Relaxation also endows the body with a vibrant and elastic quality whereby the issuance of force seems effortless. This is analogous to the bounce in a basketball. A ball with a lively bounce has been filled efficiently. It requires very little effort from a player to display its rebounding property. On the other hand, an insufficiently-filled ball is considered dead – not enough air; little to no bounce. A ball of this condition demands a great amount of exertion from an individual to deliver a satisfactory level of bounce.

To exhibit the attributes of loosening and relaxation, one must train and adhere to the concept of fongsung according to the guidance of a three-word formula: *yi* (意), *san* (伸), and *cham* (沉). Yi, or intent, initiates a calm and relaxed state throughout the body that eases tension; thereby, increasing one's awareness and alertness, and elevating one's senses and sensitivities. San, to stretch out and open up, refers to manners in which the muscles, connective tissue, and joints must be primed to establish the proper tonus that will appropriately support the practitioner's techniques. Cham, to sink, alludes to the firm root that must be established so that this condition of dynamic relaxation can be exhibited. This is an ongoing process must be developed from the start and maintained over time. Unlike riding a bicycle, it is not an activity that can be recalled with proficiency after years or even months of inactivity. Rather, it is a property that permits efficacy. One cannot ride that bicycle properly if a knee injury has been sustained. And with regard to the bicycle itself, a rusted chain or deflated tires will hamper any prospect of a decent ride. In Pak Mei Kung Fu, fongsung is acquired through conditioning exercises and continual mindful practice.

The term *fing* (捧), to throw or swing, refers to the idea that muscular kinks can literally be thrown out by exercises that open up *daai ng jit* (大五節; big 5 joints) and *siu ng jit* (小五節; small 5 joints). *Fing yiu* (捧腰), *fing sau* (捧手), and *fing geuk* (捧腳) are essential warm-up routines that prime the connective tissue of the waist/core, hands/arms, and legs, respectively. Through twining movements that achieve full extension without hyperextending the joints, tension is released and stiffness is relieved. As these sequences are performed, the big 5 joints: *kwa* (胯; inguinal crease), *yiu* (腰; waist), *bui* (背; back), *bok* (膊; shoulders), and *but* (脖; neck), and the small 5 joints: *ji* (指; fingers and toes), *wa* (踝; ankles), *sat* (膝; knees), *jau/jang* (肘; elbows), and *wun* (腕; wrists), are prepped for the smooth transfer of ging, or issuing force, throughout the body. In combination with static stretches, this dynamic movement provides the practitioner with a comprehensive method of relaxing the muscles and loosening the joints which enables the body to maneuver its parts in an optimal manner. This entire process, when trained correctly over time, moves from a voluntary activity to an involuntary accomplishment. Only after this is achieved can a practitioner truly begin to train in Pak Mei methods.

It is important to note that different circumstances will necessitate modifications to one's fostering of fongsung. If one is employed in an occupation where there is constant muscular exertion such as construction or a moving service, supplemental massage therapy is required to assist in the relaxation and loosening process. Also, during the winter months, it is advisable to dedicate at least double the amount of time to undo the stiffness that results from the body's response to cold weather conditions. Furthermore, as the body matures with age, it is essential to preserve its elasticity and muscle tone to ease the course of daily activities and to lessen the possibilities of accidental injuries. Even more efforts toward the commitment to fongsung are encouraged to support this stage of life. To this end, fongsung is not only a key component of martial arts training, but it is an indispensable aspect of a good quality of life.

Chyun Ging

Inch strength, or *chyun ging* (寸勁), assumes multiple meanings in Pak Mei Kung Fu.

As a measure of one's progress and development in the process of training Chinese martial arts, chyun ging refers to the manner in which the body changes toward a more refined state. Inch by inch from the ground upward, the body is transformed into a fully integrated structure capable of issuing martial force in a maximized manner. Each inch in this context does not refer to a specific time frame that it takes to achieve this feat. Instead, it suggests that each person's progress is a personal one that is measured in progressive increments when one's training is consistent and the instruction is correct.

In terms of combat, there are two characteristics of chyun that are critical to the execution and production of martial power. For a majority of the lay population, close-range fighting is an unfamiliar and uncomfortable distance. Hence, the ability to apply effective striking, kicking, clinching, joint-manipulation, or throwing within inches of an opponent's bridge or body is vital to one's success in close-range combat. The concept of chyun in this case refers to the idea that with limited space, one must employ the proper body methods that will infiltrate an opponent's defenses and create a relentless offense, one that will eventually overwhelm and overtake the opponent. Within Pak Mei Kung Fu, it is believed that the continuous pressuring and redirection through touch-sensitive techniques will in due course cause the opponent to commit a mistake that can ultimately lead to the end of the altercation. Not giving the opponent even an inch to respond or retaliate can stifle his physical attack and stun his intent. Correspondingly, having the skill to apply functional techniques within just inches of an opponent's structure amplifies the potency of one's attacks against an opponent inexperienced with in-fighting.

While luk ging and sei noi biu ging, as they were addressed earlier, serve as the foundations for close-range combat, chyun ging expresses a body method that stores potential inches at the joints to be released throughout one's techniques. Effective striking typically requires some degree of distance by way of chambering or a wind-up to produce a forceful impact. To compensate for the distance, the twining and torsion that is present throughout each movement essentially recreates the length in a compressed manner that a chamber or wind-up would normally deliver. The inch in this instance refers to the coils of length that are hidden within the twisting and turning motions that are facilitated at the joints. Each turn will either store or release the energy that is present within each coil of movement.

An inch can amount to everything in close-range combat.

New York Pak Mei Kung Fu
Cultural Preservation Association

CHAPTER THREE

Martial Concepts

"A good plan is like a road map: it shows the final destination and usually the best way to get there."

- H. Stanley Judd,

Author

Three, or saam (三), is a frequently occurring number not only in Chinese martial arts, but in Chinese culture in general. In the context of yin and yang, three is considered yang – an auspicious number; in reference to the Five Elements, it assumes the form of the wood element; with regard to its directional designation, three is east. The groupings of three for the most part have been modeled after the ubiquitous trinity of heaven-earth-mankind – representing the harmonious union of the three primary constituents of the universe.

Traditionally, poetic phrases and popular proverbs came in the form of threes. One classical set of elementary phrases was: 天有三寶: 日, 月, 星; 地有三寶: 水, 火, 風; 人有三寶: 神, 氣, 精 (*Tin yau saam bou: yat, yut, sing; dei yau saam bou: seui, fo, fung; yan yau saam bou: san, hei, jing*) – Heaven has 3 treasures: the sun, moon, and stars; earth has 3 treasures: water, fire, and wind; mankind has 3 treasures: spirit, breath, and essence. Those fortunate enough to enter into a formal education would be introduced to the academia via these time-honored sayings. As it can be seen, the concept of heaven-earth-mankind is deeply ingrained in Chinese traditions from childhood onto adulthood. From an ancient era to modern times, this trinity pervades the customs and culture of Chinese society.

As such, the influence of heaven-earth-mankind has inspired many principles and concepts in the form of three. For instance, *saam gaau* (三教), the three teachings, represents the three main philosophies underlying the Chinese mindset: Taoism, Buddhism and Confucianism; *saam saang* (三生), or the three births, refers to the ancient belief in reincarnation giving rise to three lives: past, present and future. Therefore, it is no surprise that concepts in terms of three are pervasive in Chinese martial arts. The three body shapes, three doors, three paths, and three gates all refer to effective fighting concepts and strategies within Pak Mei Kung Fu.

Saam Ying

Saam ying (三形) refers to the three primary body shapes that are employed when executing Pak Mei techniques. The *ying* (形), or shape, of a practitioner's body enables calculated and effectual techniques to be executed. Shape in this context refers to the appearance of the practitioner's postures that will facilitate qi transport which in turn produces the appropriate ging to maximize the effectiveness of techniques.

The three categories of fighting shapes are: *bin* (扁), *bok* (薄) and *yun* (圓). The strategic functions of each shape are to simultaneously neutralize, control, and counter an opponent's attacks. A practitioner is able to capitalize on offensive opportunities during defensive situations by exploiting the breaches in an opponent's attacks while reinforcing defensive tactics through the employment of an advantageous posture.

Bin: Flat Shape

Bin (扁), or flat, makes reference to the slanted positioning of the practitioner's torso angled in the direction of the opponent. Through its angular posture, the flat shape minimizes the map of vital areas where an opponent can attack while simultaneously maintaining optimal leverage to launch a counteroffensive.

The leading side defends the visceral region by narrowing the field of vital targets that an opponent would seek to expose and exploit on an individual. The abdominal and thoracic cavities are possibly the most sensitive areas in the body since they house the essential internal organs that sustain life functions. Full exposure of the frontal part of the body forms a wide area to cover from a defensive perspective. As the torso shifts into an angular position, the side toward the rear of the practitioner is concealed from the opponent. Therefore, the practitioner has effectively created a slimmer upper body structure, or flat shape, to naturally guard at least one side of the visceral cavities while pursuing a counter maneuver against an attack. This in turn forces the opponent to work harder in order to gain entry to either of the practitioner's particular sides.

Offensively, the leading side provides supplemental leverage to support deflecting techniques. The flat shape assists the extremities in a manner comparable to a wedge – securing, levering, and splitting in an intrusive and disruptive way. In Pak Mei Kung Fu, a block does not merely prevent the penetration of an attack, but more so, serves to injure the opponent in the process. An elementary level block typically employs the hard hitting force of direct blocks whereby limbs knock against limbs. An individual using this method of blocking risks personal injury, particularly if the opponent is larger or more conditioned and experienced. An intermediate form of blocking involves neutralizing the attack in a deflecting manner. This requires the practitioner to sense the opponent's force, harmonize with it, and lead the opponent toward a compromising position. In an advanced method of blocking, the practitioner simultaneously intercepts and attacks with the blocking limb within the same action. The torsion force within Pak Mei practices facilitates the neutralization and penetration of techniques within this advanced blocking formula supported by the flat shape.

Bok: Thin Shape

Bok (薄) means thin. Within Pak Mei Kung Fu, bok refers to the perpendicular positioning of the practitioner's body as the individual faces an opponent.

While bin is the shape that supports a head-to-head confrontation, bok is the shape that reinforces a side-to-head encounter. In other words, the practitioner confronts the opponent with the side of the body as the opponent faces the practitioner with a frontal posture – a flank to front confrontation.

This thin shape maximizes defensive positioning while also amplifying the strength of the force that is issued into a technique. Resting on a sitting stance, better described as an abridged horse stance with the practitioner's weight equally distributed between both legs, bok ying is able to completely shield one side of the body and the vital points found on the abdominal and thoracic cavities from the opponent. While one flank of the practitioner is protected, the side facing the opponent also limits the options that the opponent has to penetrate. The thinner the practitioner's vital areas present themselves to the opponent, the less likelihood of being struck. Simultaneous defensive and offensive hand skills address the protection of the flank facing the opponent. *Chin tau* (千頭) – one thousand character head, guards against possible throat attacks by tucking the chin. This decreases the size of the throat area to the opponent, thwarting attacks to this vital region.

The forces supporting specific hand techniques, baat ging, in combination with bok ying are augmented by the structure of the thin shape. In bok ying, the body's weight is constructively incorporated into the effectiveness of a technique. The extremities, the arms and hands, typically issue the force when a technique is applied. When the weight of the practitioner is integrated into a technique, the strength of the same technique will be reinforced and magnified. The strategic manipulations of the body's natural weight combined with the physics of optimizing the transference of martial force are the advantages of employing the thin shape. Typically, charging or suppressing forces are the products of bok ying.

When a practitioner moves into a thin shape, the transition can aggressively close the distance between the practitioner and the opponent or serve to reinforce a subduing technique. The charging force propelled by bok ying can effectively penetrate an opponent's unguarded midsection with the proper timing and opportunity. On the other hand, the rooting of this particular stance in conjunction with the pressure of the practitioner's leading flank can successfully sink and subdue an opponent whose balance and stability have been compromised.

Yun: Round Shape

Yun (圓) means round. Within the context of saam ying, yun refers to the curves and arcs found particularly in the shoulders, back and chest that form this round structure. The uniqueness of this shape is the result of the breathing mechanics that support the techniques as well as the synchronized methods of defense and attack that are trademarks of Pak Mei Kung Fu. Yun ying guards against high impact strikes and also extends the range of techniques that can be executed by the practitioner.

With regard to inherent defensive principles, the curves and arcs of the round shape configuration act as structural braces that will dissipate the impact of powerful attacks. The round shape can divert and disperse the energy of a strike from an opponent throughout the entire structure rather than take on the full brunt of a blow. The rounded shoulders, the flexed back, and the concaved chest collectively assist in the rerouting of an opponent's energy to decrease the practitioner's potential for injury from the force of a stronger or more powerful opponent. Very similar to the tuck position that is used defensively by boxers, the round shape also protects the practitioner's abdominal and thoracic cavities by enclosing the vital areas within a wall of arms, elbows and hands ready to envelop and assail an incoming attack. To further layer the defensive aspect of the round shape, the torsion and twining motions indigenous to Pak Mei techniques enable the practitioner to deflect direct incoming strikes.

Offensively, the arcs and curves of the round shape facilitate lengthening a practitioner's reach when executing techniques. Particularly in close-quarter encounters, subtlety and proximity become critical factors in striking effectiveness. The nature of close-range combat compels a practitioner to be efficient, continuous and direct in response to an altercation. A skilled practitioner recognizes the appropriate strategy to apply in a situation as a result of experience and understanding. Attacking without the need to reset or retreat sustains the momentum of the movements and presses forward the attack. To effectively enter and attack an opponent's weak areas is considered direct. The combination of these tenets forms the core of an efficient fighting strategy. With regard to yun ying, the characteristics of the round shape are used not only to emphasize defense, but are also constructively employed as an offense both technically and strategically.

Saam Mun

Saam mun (三門), or three doors, refers to the three horizontal divisions of the body that have been designated as both regions of attack and defense. These partitioned zones outline the geography of vital areas on the body. Furthermore, they are the foundation upon which the map of finer vital points rest.

The upper door is known as *seung mun* (上門). This zone consists of the head and upper chest region. Within this door, the vital targets located on the face and the meridians running along the upper chest are the primary areas to both attack and defend. Typically, eager opponents will immediately attack this door in pursuit of landing the famous knockout blow. As a result, seung mun is generally the most guarded as well as most sought after region during a physical altercation.

The middle door is identified as *jung mun* (中門). This central zone is comprised of the body's primary internal organs. Accordingly, many sensitive points and critical cavities can be targeted within this region to cause an opponent serious injury. Conversely, due to the vulnerability of this area, a highly effective defense needs to be in place to protect the ribs and viscera of this region. Of the three doors, this sector raises the most concern due to the abundance of vital points that can harm either the opponent or the practitioner.

Saam Mun

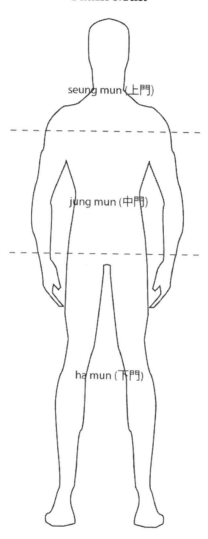

seung mun (上門)

jung mun (中門)

ha mun (下門)

Ha mun (下門) is the term used to refer to the lower door. This section is the source of the individual's foundation – the stance and footwork. While this region is primarily composed of the lower extremities, the legs, a primary vital area in this zone is the groin – in particular, the highly sensitive testes. The strategic positioning of an individual's legs throughout various stances can effectively shield the groin area from attacks. Furthermore, the mobility and maneuverability of the footwork enables the individual to evade risky situations or engage in opportune encounters. Attacks to the legs are typically designed to trip, trap or maim an individual. An experienced practitioner can open the other doors by entering through this one first.

Saam Lou

Saam lou (三路) is known as the three paths. These are the three vertical divisions that further define an individual's physical geography for both attack and defense. Two vertical lines trisect the front of the body into three equal zones.

Yau bin (右邊) is an individual's proper right flank. The limits of this zone are defined by the outline of body's outer right side and an imaginary line that drops from the middle of the right clavicle, bisecting the right rib cage, and equally dividing the leg into interior and exterior sections. The primary cavities and organs within this region are: the temple, right lung, liver, gall bladder, right hip, and exterior knee and ankle joints.

Saam Lou

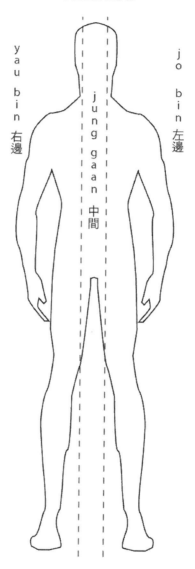

Jo bin (左邊) is an individual's proper left side. The boundaries of this region are defined by the outline of the body's outer left side and an imaginary line that drops from the middle of the left clavicle, bisecting the left rib cage, and evenly partitioning the left leg into interior and exterior segments. The primary cavities and organs housed within this zone are: the temple, left lung, part of the stomach, spleen, left hip, and exterior knee and ankle joints.

Jung gaan (中間) is an individual's middle section. This zone is bounded by the two vertical lines that define the right and left regions. Within this middle area, vital cavities are found along the entire route of a line that would perfectly bisect this section. The primary organs found in this zone are: the heart; parts of: the lungs, liver, and stomach; the large intestine; and the small intestine. Of the three paths of saam lou, this section maintains the most vital areas and points. As a result, many postures inherently guard this path and most techniques are built around defending this zone while simultaneously penetrating an opponent's doors and paths.

Saam Gwaan

Saam gwaan (三關), or three gates, refers to the concept that the arm is divided into three sections. Each section is defined by a major joint of articulation: the wrist, elbow and shoulder. The wrist is identified as *tau gwaan* (頭關), or first gate. The elbow is labeled *yi gwaan* (二關), second gate, and the shoulder is known as *saam gwaan* (三關), or third gate.

An individual's ging travels through each of these gates, or stages, during the application of a technique that involves the arms. In the fashion of a countdown, the force produced by luk ging and directed by sei noi biu ging travels from the waist up through the torso into the shoulders – the third gate, the elbows – the second gate, and the wrists – the first gate: 3...2...1.

Saam Gwaan

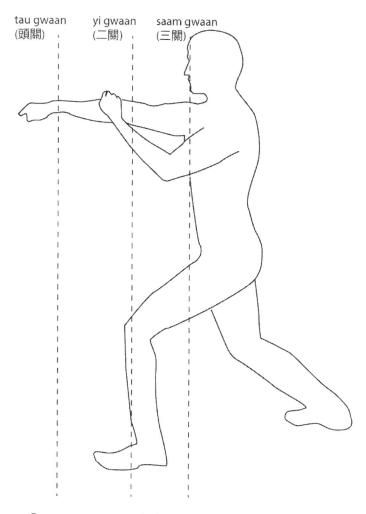

tau gwaan
(頭關)

yi gwaan
(二關)

saam gwaan
(三關)

Saam gwaan defines the range by which an individual can effectively execute a technique. The range or distance between two individuals dictates the type of body movement that will be required to maximize an attack. A distance beyond the maximum reach of the opponent's arms may mean that kicks will be employed. A feint is typically used to gauge a sense of range or to set up the challenger for a more opportune attack. At extremely close ranges, elbows or even shoulders become the main anatomical weapons.

If any of these gates within saam gwaan is obstructed, the technique's effectiveness and original intent may be both hampered and altered, respectively. For instance, if a straight punch is thrown toward an opponent and it is blocked at the wrist – tau gwaan, the force of the practitioner's punch has been successfully obstructed, or blocked. While this technique was originally intended to be a straight punch, the block has altered its course. Since the second and third gates have not been obstructed and are still operational, the elbow or shoulder can press toward the opponent, assuming a permutation of the original straight punch and capitalizing on what was initially halted by the opponent's block. Immobilizing, tying up, breaking, or combinations of these tactics have been developed in Pak Mei Kung Fu through a study of the three gates of the arm. An endless number of effective strategies can emerge from a mastery of saam gwaan.

CHAPTER FOUR

Animal Essences

"Reason is the natural order of truth; but imagination is the organ of meaning."

- C.S. Lewis,

Author (1898 – 1963)

The influence and inspiration of animals are prevalent throughout Chinese martial arts. As creatures of the natural environment, the behaviors and characteristics of animals are instinctive and adapted to their surroundings. In the spirit of stimulating one's imagination or enhancing one's survival, the observation, examination and emulation of animals have played a large role in the tradition of Chinese martial arts. From China's most famous physician, *Hua To's Ng Kam Hei* (華陀: 五禽戲), or Five Animal Sports exercises to specific systems of self-defense dedicated to the majestic white crane, the predatory praying mantis, the agile monkey, and scores of other creatures, animals have provided endless sources of ideas and augmentation to the pursuits of both scholars and martial practitioners alike.

The Five Shaolin Animals

For the most part, systems, styles and family methods of Southern Chinese martial arts have typically traced their folk origins to the Shaolin Temple. Within the walls of this celebrated martial sanctuary, the Five Shape Boxing Methods were said to train and enhance the martial practitioner's physique, psyche and spirit. Each shape or pattern was modeled after the characteristics of five principle animals: The dragon, snake, crane, tiger, and leopard. Traditionally, each animal trained a specific quality:

- *Lung* (龍), or dragon, emphasizes *jing* (精; spirit).

- *Se* (蛇), or snake, is associated with *qi* (氣; *hei* in Cantonese).

- *Hok* (鶴), or crane, is related to *ging* (勁; force).

- *Fu* (虎), or tiger, corresponds to *gwat* (骨; bones).

- *Paau* (豹), or leopard, is linked to *gei* (肌; muscles).

These five particular animals have conventionally been associated with Shaolin Temple folklore pertaining to Southern Chinese martial arts and have managed to make their way into the patterns, behavior, and spirit of nearly all martial methods of Southern China. As forms of both inspiration and emulation, each animal has a unique set of characteristics that, when combined as a whole, completes a Southern practitioner's sense of the essence of the art.

Within the Pak Mei tradition, it is said that the Shaolin ancestors, or immortals, transmitted the shapes of the dragon, snake and crane; and, Pak Mei conveyed the qualities of the tiger and the leopard. As a martial style allegedly passed down from one of Shaolin's most legendary, mythical and controversial figures, Pak Mei Kung Fu employs the essence of each of the five animals with an emphasis on the tiger and the leopard. The contribution of each animal as it has been incorporated or expressed in Pak Mei Kung Fu is uniquely tailored to assist a practitioner in achieving the qualities and characteristics that are beyond human limits.

Lung: Dragon

The dragon is traditionally considered the most powerful of all animals. Its superior qualities are products of ancient inspiration as well as exaggerated imagination. The dragon's physical behavior, or *lung hang* (龍行), and supple waist (龍腰), *lung yiu*, are this animal's primary attributes that are emphasized in Pak Mei Kung Fu.

To move in the dragon's manner and to attain a similar waist action are considered essential elements in the training and development of Pak Mei Kung Fu. The dragon's coiling body, compressing and releasing through the clouds, is the model that the practitioner's core and waist must emulate to successfully execute rising and sinking motions. In the same manner that this spiraling motion is the dragon's source of movement, the practitioner's waist and core region must combine to initiate the activity of the upper body's movements. The waist directs the motion that the upper body will undertake, leading the ging from the body's legs to its upper extremities.

The dragon presses the offensive with cross-pattern footwork and entangling arm engagement. On the retreat, the dragon lures its opponent into a compromising position using the same tactics that are employed on the offensive. The key to the mastery of this creature's effective techniques are found in the command of one's body connection. The way in which its body behaves is mythically instinctual. This is the quality that the practitioner needs to emulate, internalize and master.

Se: Snake

The snake is one of the most respected and feared reptiles, achieving its reverence primarily through the awe, and fear, of its speed and precision. While these are its most observable and obvious characteristics, the less apparent attribute of this animal is the manner in which its speed and precision are derived – through the optimized flow of qi which materializes in the form of ging, enabling the speed and precision to occur.

The muscles and supporting tissue of a practitioner's physiology need to follow the snake's relaxed and flexible body. Qi travels in an unobstructed and fluid fashion in the presence of relaxation and calmness. The snake naturally assumes such a state prior to exercising its speed and accuracy during an attack. When it is stated that, of the five animals, the snake is associated with the training of qi, suppleness, relaxation and calmness are the qualities the practitioner needs to learn in order for techniques to be effective.

Within Pak Mei Kung Fu, there are techniques which are considered *duk se* (毒蛇), or literally poisonous snake techniques. What makes a technique venomous is the combination of speed, accuracy and stealth. Speed enables the technique to be quick and lively which raises the likelihood of penetration and effectiveness. Accuracy is necessary to strike intended cavities, meridians and vital targets to stun, disable or even kill. Stealth provides an aspect of invisibility and an element of surprise which, when coupled with speed and accuracy, creates the potential for lethal techniques to be realized. Pak Mei Kung Fu's *duk sau* (毒手), or poison hands, are directly influenced by and derived from these exceptional qualities of the snake.

Hok: Crane

Of all the species of birds in Chinese culture, the crane has been associated with longevity due to its proactive stance toward self-preservation and protection as observed in nature. Unlike some other creatures in nature, the crane relies on ging rather than lik in its actions. It emphasizes refined force and finesse rather than sheer strength and brute muscle. The crane's mastery of balance enables it to maintain its own center while stealing its opponent's foundation. Through its nearly flawless evasive maneuvers and the skillful timing to strike at the opportune moment, the crane is able to defend itself quite capably against predators.

Within Pak Mei Kung Fu, the crane's influence is subtle yet inherent in many aspects of the system's principles and theories. The crane's allusion to longevity is akin to the practitioner's pursuits in Pak Mei Kung Fu. The Taoist aspect of subscribing to The Way and lengthening one's lifespan through self-cultivation is the rarely divulged aspect of the art that balances its emphasis on ferocity and relentlessness. Understanding how to equalize the fire-water qi relationship in the body and balancing the intense training and fierce performances with the relaxed states of slow boxing and seated breath training are the primary ways that most Pak Mei practitioners avoid premature degeneration and promote rejuvenation. With regard to martial power, ging is emphasized over lik in the same fashion that the crane prefers the use of cultivated force over sheer muscular strength. Additionally, in terms of martial strategy the Pak Mei practitioner relies on a sense of timing in sync with offensively evasive tactics to overcome an opponent much along the same lines as a crane fending off an attack in nature.

Fu: Tiger

In Chinese culture, the tiger is a symbol of strength and ferocity. It is believed that the strength of an animal is derived from its bones – the stronger the animal, the stronger its bones must be. This includes the muscles, tendons and ligaments that are affiliated with the bones. As a result, the tiger is associated with bone strengthening according to the Shaolin tradition pertaining to the Five Animals, or Five Shaolin Shapes. Since the marrow of the bones sustains and supports the body's essential functions, which in turn defines physical power, the best animal to emulate was the tiger. It is in this manner that the tiger came to become one of the Five Shaolin Shapes.

With regard to status, the title of a tiger is typically bestowed upon famous warriors or champion fighters. *Guangdong Sap Fu* (廣東十虎; Guangdong or Canton's Ten Tigers), *Dunggong Maang Fu* (東江猛虎; Dunggong's Fierce Tiger), and *Dunggong Saam Fu* (東江三虎; Dunggong's Three Tigers) are just a few examples of the prestigious tiger designation. A famous Chinese proverb states that a mountain cannot have two tigers on it – making reference to the tiger's territoriality, dominance and aggression. These characteristics are the tiger's primary qualities that are emphasized in Pak Mei Kung Fu.

Fu bui (虎背) or tiger back refers to the strength that is needed to appropriately command this body part. As one of the essential components of luk ging, the back needs to be firm yet flexible to assist in the production and execution of force – ging. The practitioner's back needs to embody the likeness of a tiger in a predatory position – ready to pounce on its prey.

As one of nature's most fearsome mammals, the tiger is well-known for its stalking and hunting abilities. *Fu bou* (虎步), or tiger stepping, imitates the mammal's advancing movements and retreating patterns – regulating the range and controlling the rate of attack. This form of footwork facilitates the smooth transition of movements without compromising the integrity of the practitioner's stance or balance in the same mannerisms and cadences of a stalking tiger in nature.

Paau: Leopard

The leopard, or panther, is a much leaner member of the family of large predatory cats. Its strength stems from sheer muscle which translates to speed more so than power due to its sleek physical design. According to the Shaolin canon pertaining to the five animals of Southern methods of mou seut, the leopard is noted for its muscularity, speed and quickness.

While both the tiger and the leopard are hunters, their styles are different due to their physical makeup and the environments in which they exist. Since leopards can climb trees and are comfortable at different height levels, its attacking methods are modified to suit its body and environmental conditions. The leopard is swift and agile. This enables it to adopt more angular approaches and attacks in a variety of ways.

In Pak Mei Kung Fu, practitioners vary in size, shape and personal preferences. While the leopard conveys a sense of muscular strength and speed within the Southern Shaolin tradition, it addresses the practitioner on a personal level in Pak Mei Kung Fu. The leopard's speed and agility are highly appropriate for a practitioner whose build is lean and whose frame is small relative to the average person. Strategically, angular attacks and evasions are more productive against a much larger and stronger opponent. From the vantage point of height, a tall practitioner can follow the model of a leopard in the trees – alert with a sense of readiness and attuned to the tactical advantage that height provides. The leopard's influence differentiates its inspiration to suit the needs of the practitioner.

Ying: Eagle

Aside from the classical Southern Shaolin Five Animals, the eagle, or *ying* (鷹), is also emphasized in Pak Mei Kung Fu, particularly in the patterns or techniques that have been imported to expand and augment the core Pak Mei training sets. The eagle is renowned for its seizing prowess, keen vision, and predatory instincts. Within Pak Mei Kung Fu, all of these qualities are essential in providing the practitioner with a comprehensive foundation to both reach and the raise the individual's level of skill.

The eagle appears in many methods and forms in Pak Mei Kung Fu. The form *Sap Ji Kyun* (十字拳) – Ten Character (shape) Boxing, had originally been called *Sap Ji Ying Jaau Kau Da* (十字鷹爪扣打), or Ten Character (shape) Eagle Claw Knocking Strike. *Ying Jaau Nim Kiu* (鷹爪黏橋), or Eagle Claw Sticking Bridge, is Cheung Lai Chuen's version of *Lung Ying Mo Kiu* (龍形摩橋) from the Dragon Style Kung Fu system – one of his foundational martial arts.

In each form, the eagle's claw is emphasized as the principle method of seizing and capturing. Depending on the practitioner's lineage, there are two versions of the eagle claw that can be employed in Pak Mei Kung Fu. The *ying jaau* (鷹爪) – eagle claw, can be formed by holding the four fingers of the clawing hand closely together, as opposed to the *fu jaau* (虎爪) – tiger claw, whereby the four fingers are spread apart. The supportive fingers of the eagle claw serve to reinforce the strength of the grip by forming a single, solid seizing grab. Whereas the fu jaau covers more surface area to facilitate tearing and ripping, the ying jaau is generally employed for seizing and crushing or setting up for a subsequent technique.

Another version of the ying jaau involves a three finger grip that uses the index and middle fingers and thumb to form the grab. This variation, which physically emulates the eagle's talons, is typically used by those practitioners whose primary finger strength lies within the digits of this particular hand formation. Whether it is a practitioner's natural proclivity or personal preference, this variation of the ying jaau serves the same functional purpose as its four-fingered clenching counterpart – to seize, crush, or set up for a finishing technique.

Fu Paau Seung Ying: Tiger Leopard Paired Shapes

It is interesting to note that of the Five Shaolin Animals, two are mammals from the family of large predatory cats. *Fu paau seung ying* (虎豹雙形), or tiger leopard paired shapes, makes reference to the notion that of the Five Shaolin Animals, the tiger and the leopard were selected to receive the most emphasis within Pak Mei Kung Fu.

The relationship that the tiger and the leopard share in Pak Mei Kung Fu is analogous to the yin and yang dynamic, whereby the tiger is yang and the leopard is yin. Both animals convey a comprehensive view of aggressive and predatory behavior. The spirit of the tiger's ferocity and fearlessness and essence of the leopard's speed and tenacity are the keys to the Pak Mei practitioner's successful fighting nature. Without these guiding characteristics, techniques are merely movements; strategies are merely plans; and, ging is simply an aimless force. The tiger and the leopard influences transform these fighting principles into successful applications indicative of Pak Mei Kung Fu. As the instincts of these predators are incorporated, the techniques are infused with intent and intensity. This intensive and aggressive aspect, however, must be tempered and refined so that it does not overtake one's sense of morality and civility; but, can be called upon during times of urgency to successfully resolve a situation and be restored to its proper place in training, understanding and implementation. Ideally, the practitioner should be able to treat this ferocious and relentless spirit as a switch – turning it on when needed and shutting it off when done.

With regard to strategic execution, the tiger's strength and directness is balanced by the leopard's speed and angular approach. The ripping and tearing actions of the tiger are facilitated by its fully committed and straightforward attacks. This is considered an actively yang approach. Strength in this regard is defined as power that is so strong that it cannot be compromised or diverted. Relying on finesse and speed, the leopard emphasizes a more yin approach relative to its tiger counterpart. Quick changes in movement or altering angular attacks are characteristic of the leopard. It employs its speed in a manner that accommodates movement changes rather than powering directly toward its opponent or prey. These two perspectives integrating the tiger and leopard's unique influences provide the practitioner with an array of approaches to counter an opponent's attacks in a controlled yet aggressive manner.

CHAPTER FIVE

Training Methods

"All great success and achievement is preceded and accompanied by hard, hard work. When in doubt, try harder. And if that doesn't work, try harder still."

– Brian Tracy

In Pak Mei Kung Fu, *lin gung* (練功) – or training [one's] skills, consists of conditioning exercises, forms practice, and technique usage to ensure that a comprehensive representation of the system is properly passed onto the next generation of practitioners. While a practitioner is engaged in these aspects of the martial art, the essential elements of Pak Mei Kung Fu can be developed and grasped; when a practitioner is wedded to the training and development of Pak Mei practice, the journey toward martial mastery is guided by five main objectives that traditionally define martial skill in Pak Mei Kung Fu. The attainment of *chung sau* (重手; heavy hands), *nim sau* (黏手; sticking hands), *tau sau* (偷手; stealing hands), *ging jaak ging* (驚擲勁; startled tossing force), and *duk sau* (毒手; poison hands) have characteristically distinguished combative mastery from generalized martial excellence within Pak Mei Kung Fu. The following sections will discuss the details associated with all of the aforementioned areas.

Cheui: Conditioning the Fist; Training the Punch

While *kyun* (拳) is the expression used for fist in Cantonese, *cheui* (搥) is used to represent a punch or strike. The former indicates what the configuration is; the latter informs what it does. In Pak Mei Kung Fu, cheui is typically used to represent the standard fist that is used for a punch. The different forms of the basic cheui in Pak Mei Kung Fu include: *ping cheui* (平搥; level punch), *kau cheui* (扣搥; knocking punch [with the knuckles and the back of the fist]), *saam gok cheui* (三角搥; 3 corner punch [with the points of the knuckles]), and *pek cheui* (劈搥; splitting punch [with the outer ridge of the fist]).

The mechanics of powerful punching is trained through standard striking drills and formalized routines. The conditioning of powerful punches is trained by striking the *sa baau* (沙包), or sand bag, followed by the application of a traditional herbal strengthening liniment, *dit da chou* (跌打醋; fall and strike vinegar). Sand bags are placed flat on a stand as well as mounted on a wall. Different areas of the fist are typically conditioned on the two bag arrangements. In a more dynamic routine, a hanging weighted sand bag is trained by two individuals. Standing on each side of the bag, each practitioner alternates between blocking with the forearms and punching with the fists. The swinging motion simulates the liveliness of an opponent, and the density of the bag enables one to strike without reservation since the bag will not sustain the injuries that an actual person would under the same intense impact force.

The hardening of bones through the ancient Asian practice of sa baau training is substantiated by the Western theory known as Wolff's Law, based upon the findings of 19th Century surgeon Julius Wolff and associate Jacques Mathieu Delpech. Also known as Delpech's Law, Wolff's Law states that structural or functional changes of bones will result in alterations to their form. In other words, calcium deposits reinforce traumatized and micro-fractured bone, thereby increasing the density of the bone. The bones become stronger due to the calcium reinforcements. Dit da chou ensures proper circulation and enhances the healing process.

Fung Ngaan Cheui: The Phoenix-Eye Fist

Fung ngaan cheui (鳳眼搥) is the term used to describe the specialized fist formation that utilizes the proximal interphalangeal joint of the index finger as the primary anatomical attacking hardware typically used to strike soft tissue and vital nerve points. As a striking tool, the phoenix-eye fist is used to penetrate cavities and points on the body that can cause mild to severe reactions. The row of three knuckles adjacent to the protruding joint can also be used to simultaneously strike the surrounding target area. As a gouging or grinding implement, the adjoining knuckles can dig and scrape the surrounding tissue area that the phoenix-eye has penetrated to widen the range of damage that can be caused by the strike.

Deng cheui (釘搥), or nail strike, names a collection of striking methods that extend the range of striking positions and surfaces of the phoenix-eye fist formation. For instance, the back of the fist can be used to prime a target area before both the extended section and joint of the phoenix-eye penetrates the intended point. It is important to note that a number of factors including striking force, positioning, timing, accuracy, and the opponent's – as well as the practitioner's preexisting conditioning, will contribute to the overall effectiveness of strikes using this particular fist formation.

Two approaches to training this specialized fist include physical conditioning and accuracy exercises. The physical toughening of the phoenix-eye fist also incorporates the use of striking the sa baau with an emphasis on the extended joint. The eye of the phoenix is further conditioned using the *yat lik* (日曆), or calendar method. The traditional Chinese calendar is a 365 page hanging almanac with paper quality that is similar to the pages of a public phone book. The preference for this training apparatus was based upon the principle that a certain elasticity or cushion provided by the pages of the calendar simulated the soft tissue areas of the human body. While the sand bag trains and conditions the striking method, the Chinese calendar develops the gouging and grinding aspects of the phoenix-eye fist.

Targets will typically be sketched onto the training equipment to increase the practitioner's sense of accuracy. These sites will begin with bull's-eye targets for novices and progress to pinpoint marks for advanced practitioners. As the degree of difficulty increases, the practitioner's focus, force and intensity must increase as well.

One of the more challenging training methods for the phoenix-eye fist is to pierce a point on a single sheet of paper suspended on a string. After the practitioner has successfully trained in the conditioning of the phoenix-eye formation with the sand bag and wall calendar, the subtle and stealthy characteristics of the phoenix-eye fist must be learned. Pinpointing and piercing a target on a freely hanging sheet of paper requires not only accuracy, but finesse – a dimension that is unique to this method of training. The breeze generated by the force of a fast strike can move the sheet of paper in the same fashion that an opponent will react in response to a telegraphed technique. However, a comparable penetrating yet subtle force can pierce the hanging target in an undetected and alternatively effective manner.

The comprehensive conditioning and marksmanship that a practitioner develops through these training methods fully prepare the individual for the practical possibilities of using the phoenix-eye fist.

Biu Ji: Thrusting Fingers

Biu ji (鏢指), or thrusting fingers, refers to a category of offensive techniques using a full set of straightened fingers to attack the body's vital points or penetrate an opponent's guard. This spear hand formation is typically used to strike the eyes or throat of an individual's seung mun, or upper region. Attacks to vital points on the trunk of an opponent's body such as the stomach or rib cage using biu ji are classified as *saat gim* (殺劍), or killing swords, noted for their piercing capacity.

As a feint, the biu ji can be used to mislead the opponent by concealing the actual technique within a sudden spear hand attack. As the biu ji entices the opponent to commit to a counter maneuver, a lethal technique can be launched against another unguarded region of the opponent's body. *Mou ying geuk* (無影腳) – literally a no shadow leg [attack], better known as the shadowless kick, employs a high feint to distract the opponent in the upper region while a simultaneous kick to the groin or legs is launched to the lower door, or ha mun. While the opponent is preoccupied by the biu ji, the kick has a greater opportunity to penetrate vital targets or disable the lower extremities. This is the same strategy made famous by the *Hung Ga* (洪家) Kung Fu master *Wong Fei Hung* (黃飛鴻).

Conditioning for this specialized hand formation comes in the form of mung beans and sand training. *Luk dau* (綠荳), or literally green beans, are dried mung beans that are placed in a container deep enough to accommodate finger thrusts up to the wrists. Dehydrated beans are used to prevent undue exposure to moisture that can seep into the skin during hand training and lead to eventual arthritis and rheumatism later in life according to the tenets of Traditional Chinese Medicine. Thrusts are vigorous yet adhere to the principles of yin and yang, whereby the actions alternate between soft and hard states – relaxed en route toward the container of beans, and firm upon contact with the beans. Alternately, a container filled with sand is used in the same manner to expand the range of responsiveness that the fingers will experience when executing techniques with this hand formation.

Jeung: The Eight Primary Palms

Jeung (掌), or palm, represents the group of open-hand strikes frequently used in Pak Mei Kung Fu. While the term palm typically refers to the interior surface of the hand from the wrist to the bottom of the fingers, jeung within a martial capacity encompasses all areas of the hand including the back, sides and fingers of an open hand. The extensive striking surfaces of jeung are manifested by different hand formations that produce a variety of offensive possibilities. Within Pak Mei Kung Fu, eight primary palm compositions are employed: *gok* (角), *yun* (軟), *teui* (推), *ding* (頂), *paak* (拍), *kap* (吸), *sip* (攝), and *paan* (攀).

Gok jeung, or corner palm, is an attacking palm using the lower outer edge of the hand to target areas located within an opponent's seung mun – upper door, particularly the neck and jaw. Yun jeung, or soft palm, employs the back of the hand to strike pressure points or sensitive areas positioned on an opponent's head or neck – again, targets housed in the upper sector of the body. Teui jeung refers to a pushing palm that typically uses aggressive shoves or forceful strikes to an opponent's jung mun, or middle door. Ding jeung, or upward-facing offensive palm, is primarily directed at the internal organs located in the lower half of the middle door.

These four palms are inherently offensive and are characteristically used in conjunction with a supporting defensive hand.

The remaining four palms are generally designed to be defensive but are used in an offensive capacity. In other words, the palms in this particular category will defend a practitioner while they attack the opponent. Paak jeung is a slapping or striking palm that is generally the defensive hand that accompanies its offensive counterpart. While this palm formation can be a block protecting a practitioner's upper or middle doors, its execution conveys the forceful impact of a strike. Typically, when this block protects the practitioner's upper sector, it is known as paak jeung; however, when it protects the middle door, it is better known as *kam sau* (扣手), or slapping hand. Kap jeung, or drawing inward palm, starts as an evasive technique that can dissolve an attack, actively lures in an opponent, and ends as an overpowering palm strike to the opponent's upper or middle door. Sip jeung, or absorbing palm, intercepts and deflects an incoming attack as it simultaneously strikes the weak points located within the opponent's middle door. Paan jeung, or raising palm, is intended to overwhelm an opponent's senses, counter grabs, and simultaneously attack an opponent's seung mun using the back of the hand.

Like most traditional Chinese martial arts, the palm is conditioned using the sa baau, or sand bag. The different areas of the hand that strike the bag include: the inside of the palm, the back of the hand, the outer edge of the hand, the corner of the palm, and the heel of the palm. On the sand bag apparatus, this hand conditioning regimen is typically trained in combination with closed fist strikes.

Additionally, two rather unique Pak Mei practices to test palm skills are to shatter a coconut and to extinguish a candle's flame. To assess the toughness of a Pak Mei practitioner's palms, breaking a coconut, or *da ye ji* (打椰子), is a method that was commonly used. This task requires the practitioner to be dedicated to a continuous palm conditioning schedule in conjunction with intensive qigong exercises before attempting the break. In contrast, to snuff out a candle's flame from a distance demonstrates the suppleness and finesse that is required to execute the more subtle hand methods indigenous to Pak Mei Kung Fu. To be successful with the *juk* (燭), or candle, the practitioner must achieve an advanced level of relaxation along with a mastery of body connection and force expression. This trains the softer side of the palm techniques employed in Pak Mei.

To balance the physical demands placed on the hands during sand bag training, a traditional herbal liniment is applied to prevent the premature deterioration of the hands and dexterity degeneration of the fingers. As previously mentioned in reference to conditioning the fist, dit da chou is used to strengthen the striking surfaces on the hand and to avert the threat of joint destruction from training those striking methods on the sa baau. Without the use of dit da chou, the prospect of acquiring rheumatoid arthritis or other joint-related illnesses emerging in a practitioner's later years in life is greatly increased. Moreover, the type of stress and force placed on the joints from the pounding and striking that takes place during conditioning can also lead to nerve damage and limited finger mobility. Dit da chou is designed to equalize these negative effects that can result from sand bag training and coconut breaking.

Comprehensive breathing methods employed throughout all phases of palm training address strengthening and safety from an internal perspective. During sa baau training, specific breathing patterns lead the qi to the striking areas of the hand to fortify the hand structures and to energize the force of the strikes. Prior to any physical training on the sa baau, a series of qigong exercises are practiced diligently to promote an intrinsic strengthening of the hands, particularly to protect and preserve the joints that can easily be damaged from such rigorous conditioning. Accordingly, the qigong practice is continued throughout the course of the practitioner's training regardless of hand conditioning routines to foster elasticity and flexibility within the joints.

Jaau: Eagle and Tiger Claws

The *jaau* (爪), or claw, is divided into two categories in Pak Mei Kung Fu: the eagle claw and the tiger claw. The *ying jaau* (鷹爪), or eagle claw, is primarily used for grabbing and seizing while the *fu jaau* (虎爪), or tiger claw, is customarily employed in tearing and ripping behaviors. In practice and praxis, all palms and claws are used interchangeably and are quite often used in combination with each other depending on the requirements of the situation.

With regard to training and strengthening, a specific set of routines is dedicated to developing the jaau. A different type of sa baau is used to address the grabbing and tearing actions of the claws. A manageable sand bag that can fit within a practitioner's grip trains the clutching actions and tearing motions of the claw formation. Capturing, tossing, and twisting movements are typically performed using this particular sand bag to train the timing and positioning of grabs.

Finger strengthening is traditionally trained through *fu jaau hei san* (虎爪起身), or the tiger claw push-up – literally, tiger claw raising the body. In this exercise, the practitioner is set to perform a standard push-up that rests and raises the body from the hands' claw formation. While this has been a time-honored method of training finger strength, modern sports medicine has proven that this activity is quite harmful to the finger joints since so much weight is placed on the practitioner's fingertips. In this circumstance, the long-term loss in finger dexterity tends to outweigh the short term gain of an antiquated view of finger strength training. To simulate the constricting grip of the claws, *ngaat gung* (壓功), or crushing training, is carried out using pebbles and stones. In this exercise, the practitioner takes a handful of pebbles and squeezes them in repetitive sets. This enables the practitioner to become accustomed to the sensation of clasping and gripping after a grab which leads to greater control over an opponent.

Kiu: Conditioning the Bridges

Throughout Chinese martial arts, the arms are known as bridges, or *kiu* (橋). The arms are the means by which a variety of attacks such as punching, grabbing and grappling can be made. In Pak Mei, the practitioner exploits an opponent's weaknesses via the arms when each other's bridges are engaged in combat. The arms themselves can be manipulated and attacked, exposing the opponent to more potentially dangerous tactics that are inherent in Pak Mei techniques.

To condition the arms, the exercise known as *tit luk gwan* (鐵轆滾), or iron windlass rolling, is incorporated into the training routine. An iron windlass is typically a heavy, hollow iron bar, approximately 3 feet long, that is filled with metal shot fillings or a thinner metal rod that has been housed within the exterior iron casing. In this exercise, the arms are extended in front of the body and the bar is rolled back and forth throughout the entire length of the arms. This activity is designed to toughen the arms as well as act as a weight-training apparatus.

While this activity has also been part of the Pak Mei training tradition, there are unforeseen dangers that can lead to long-term maladies. Perhaps the biggest error in judgment is to use a lead bar for its superior weight over other metals. Due to the rigorous and intimate contact of the bar with the skin during the rolling exercise, lead particles can separate from the bar, enter through a practitioner's pores, and make their way into the bloodstream. As a result, lead poisoning can occur from the exposure to this metallic element. In adults, serious health problems particularly pertaining to damage to the brain, nervous system, stomach and kidneys arise, while developmental disorders occur in children who are exposed to lead in any capacity. Along these lines, practitioners of the iron palm method using metal fillings in the highest stage of training may also have unknowingly exposed themselves to lead poisoning, leading to a premature demise. The importance of awareness and intelligence prevails over any accepted and unquestioned practices.

As a result, a more suitable alternative can be to use a bamboo pole with a sufficient diameter that will permit a rod, gravel, or sand to fit inside. The filling adds both weight and a dynamic feel to the apparatus as it rolls over sections of the arms, is propped upward, and strikes the surface of the bridges. The ends should be capped off or permanently sealed to maintain the contents within the pole. In terms of practice, a scheduled routine of set repetitions should be trained regularly followed by the application of an appropriate training or healing liniment.

Geuk: The Comprehensive Concept of the Legs

Geuk (腳), or legs, typically refers to leg tactics and kicking techniques employed in Pak Mei. The legs are viewed in three distinct modes: ma (馬; stance), bou faat (步法; footwork), and geuk.

Ma, or stance, refers to the base upon which the upper body rests. It is also one of the body's six sectors responsible for the generation of Pak Mei force. Stances not only provide stability, but also serve as traps, trips and locking mechanisms against an opponent's lower extremities. The primary stance used in Pak Mei is patterned after the phrase: *ma bat ding, ma bat baat* (馬不丁, 馬不八) – the stance is not in the shape of the character 丁 and it is not in the shape of the character 八. The stability of this stance is derived from the even distribution of the practitioner's weight between both legs and the lowering of the center of gravity to the dan tian as a result of the stance. With regard to trapping or tripping an opponent, the lead leg can execute either of these two options within the appropriate range. Leg locking maneuvers that can lead to leg breaking techniques can also be achieved from the *gwai ma* (跪馬), or kneeling stance. It is important to note that this particular stance, gwai ma, had been imported from the styles that Cheung Lai Chuen had studied prior to his apprenticeship in Pak Mei Kung Fu. Moreover, it is a stance that is found in nearly all Southern Chinese martial arts systems. The assortment of stances in Pak Mei furnishes the practitioner with a wide range of leg possibilities that can take place from the stance alone.

Footwork, known as bou faat – or literally, stepping methods, facilitates a practitioner's mobility in and out of ranges. *Bik bou* (逼步), or pressuring step, enables the practitioner to engage an opponent directly in a controlled charge. This surging step closes the distance between the practitioner and the opponent, ideally leaving the opponent with no time to react appropriately or respond effectively. In contrast, *teui bou* (退步), or retreating step, widens the distance between the practitioner and the opponent, giving the practitioner enough room to evade an attack that is too quick or too powerful. An advanced practitioner will use this step to lure an opponent into a more potentially injurious technique. A sophisticated stepping method in Pak Mei is *fu bou* (虎步), or the tiger step. In this footwork tactic, the practitioner can charge or retreat with an angular approach which can conclude in an attacking stance or lead into a kicking technique. These commonly used footwork patterns exemplify the design and mobility of the numerous stepping methods found in Pak Mei.

While geuk literally means leg, the term has become synonymous with kicks – particularly in Southern Chinese martial culture. Kicks are trained at all levels: low, medium and high; yet, applied primarily against an opponent's ha mun, or lower door. Lower leg attacks are less visible, more difficult to defend against, and safeguard a practitioner's own stance integrity. Kicks are typically trained in a progressive manner from very physical to very subtle. Rigorous kicks such as *daan fei geuk* (單飛腳; single flying kick) and *chong geuk* (闖腳; charging kick) are suitable and effective for the physically fit or youthful practitioner. Training these particular kicks early on will provide a strong foundation for the subsequent kicking techniques such as *mou ying geuk* (無形腳; no shadow kick / invisible kick) and *deng geuk* (釘腳; nail kick). As the practitioner approaches the more advanced levels of the system, kicks such as *chyun sam geuk* (穿心腳; piercing the heart kick) and *sip geuk* (攝腳; absorbing kick) are introduced and expected to be mastered in order to be truly effective. When all aspects of the legs are coordinated between stance, footwork and kicks, the geuk can be considered effective and efficient Pak Mei methods.

Conditioning of the legs comes mainly in the form of an exercise called *sou geuk* (掃腳), or sweeping leg. This requires the practitioner to sweep the inner and outer shins against bundled wooden rods that have been positioned against the wall like an opponent's leg. Wood densities should also progress from pliant to hard as the individual advances with consistent practice. As with any impact conditioning routines, the appropriate training and healing liniments need to be applied in conjunction with the training program.

Leg strengthening comes from the practice of stance, footwork and kicking combinations. Prearranged routines and repetitive sets will provide the practitioner with the opportunity to not only perform leg methods correctly, but to also train the practitioner's stamina and endurance. The stances teach the practitioner to understand body balance and to optimize weight-bearing positioning. Footwork patterns performed in lengthy sets trains both leg stamina and the instinctive ability to move in and out of ranges with a partner. Endurance is trained while perfecting kicking techniques through repetitive sets followed by partnered kicking shield and pad workouts. Supplemental activities such as jogging, jumping rope, and obstacle course training also serve to enhance a practitioner's training when personal schedules allow such opportunities.

Unique and Esoteric Practices: Iron Bridge and Neck Methods

Traditional training routines at advanced levels involve strengthening and conditioning nearly every part of the body. *Mou dai chong* (無底床), better known as the iron bridge – literally translated as the bottomless bed, requires the practitioner to rest the feet and head and shoulders on the seats of two chairs while the straightened body is supported by these areas. This method is meant to strengthen the midsection of the body while also subjecting the body to a different kind of physical stressor. As the body becomes stronger through this exercise, it is expected that the mind will also lead the body to higher states of relaxation throughout the strenuous training. As with all exercises and activities, breathing is important when performing mou dai chong. The breath should never be held in – this can cause serious physical injury as well as possible internal damage.

Hau gung (喉功), or neck achievement, entails the use of a rope fastened around the practitioner's neck to strengthen the neck muscles. Similar to a hangman's noose, the loop of the rope is lightly secured around the neck of a practitioner who is being initiated into the exercise. The practitioner responds to the external stimulus with cycles of tension and release of the neck muscles coupled with corresponding breathing patterns. As progress is achieved, the rope is adjusted accordingly – which means from light to firm with each breakthrough in resistance and training. This method of training is highly not recommended due to the extremeness of the activity and the potentially fatal result that can occur from incorrect training.

Paai Da Gung

Paai da gung (排打功) – literally clustered striking feats, is a classical conditioning method that primes the body to guard against an opponent's strikes, thereby enabling the practitioner to continue attacking while being attacked.

The most recognized terms in classical Chinese martial arts related to making the body impervious to blows are *gam jung jaau* (金鐘罩; golden bell cover) and *tit bou sam* (鐵布衫; iron shirt). To the layman, golden bell and iron shirt are often used interchangeably. Customarily, the distinction lies in the approach. Golden bell, generally a Northern Chinese form of iron body training, initiates its practice from an internal perspective with a series of breathing and stretching methods to strengthen the vital organs housed in the torso and bolster the body's connective tissues. Iron shirt, a phrase more associated with the martial arts of Southern China, begins with a physical conditioning that includes massaging, tapping, and striking different areas of the body. Ultimately, each method of training culminates with the other's initial routines – golden bell exercises will move toward striking vital areas on the body to assess the practitioner's progress while iron shirt practice will balance its physical training routines with harmonizing breathing patterns.

Within Pak Mei Kung Fu, the initial stage of paai da gung begins with *dip gwat gung* (疊骨功), literally folding bones training, more commonly called rib power. The fundamental facets of this practice are seamlessly incorporated into the *san faat* (身法), or body methods, of the individual's warm-up exercises, training of *kyun* (拳; empty-hand combat routines), or as an ancillary series. *Tan tou* (吞吐), literally to swallow and spit, defines the contraction and release of the body's core muscles and rib cage to issue martial force in an integrated, or whole-body, manner and to prime the trunk of the body for further physical conditioning. The compression of the ribs cultivates a tautness that toughens the bones and connective tissue of this sensitive region to better shield the body's internal organs from an adversary's attacks while the release of the ribs amplifies the practitioner's striking force. This pair of alternating actions must be coordinated with a properly prescribed pattern of breathing to enable the practitioner to endure and alleviate the pressures of these actions on the internal organs. A precise amount of pressure can promote a positive effect on the visceral organs by acting as a massage of sorts to clear obstructed circulatory pathways. On the other hand, improper, excessive, or forceful breathing methods can act adversely by further deteriorating already weakened organs, creating obstructions, or elevating hormones to toxic levels. A practitioner's physical and mental states of being, age, and experience are critical factors that must always be taken into consideration to avoid serious injury or delayed degenerative ailments.

Dip gwat gung is innocuously introduced by way of a stepping sequence, *haang ma* (行馬; walking the horse), that leads into the system's first fist routine, *Jik Bou Kyun* (直步拳; straight stepping form), to facilitate the foundational features of dip gwat gung. While walking the horse trains the practitioner to aggressively employ *bik bou* (逼步) – the pressuring step, it simultaneously introduces the beginner to the sinking and rising dynamics of tan tou which is eventually incorporated into the combative movements native to the system.

The intermediate stage of paai da gung is when the actual physical conditioning takes place. In reality, there is a set sequence, but not necessarily a set time frame such as 100 days of tapping, 100 weeks of striking, or 100 months of apparatus conditioning that can be followed. The pace of one's progress in paai da gung is not the priority; the close attention to the body's responses to such training is. The practitioner begins with clusters of taps to areas throughout the body such as the chest and neck to assess the status and strength of vital targets. Massages are then applied to those same areas to alleviate the inflammation and tension that can accumulate from the contact. On average, after a period of three months, the practitioner moves on to light striking with the outer ridge of the hand.

There are 9 pairs of points that are primed in paai da gung:

Paai Da Gung

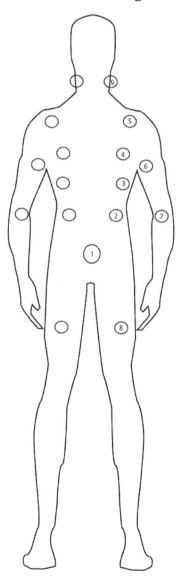

Trunk:

1 - *dan tian* (丹田; *daan tin* in Cantonese)

2 - *zhang men* (章門; *jeung mun*)

3 - *qi men* (期門; *kei mun*)

4 - *jiang tai* (將臺; *jeung toi*)

5 - *jian jing* (肩井; *gin jing*)

Extremities:

6 - *pi ru* (譬儒; *pei yu*)

7 - *qu chi* (曲池; *kuk chi*)

8 - *bai hai* (白海; *baak hoi*)

9 - *sai jiao* (腮角; *soi gok*)

With the exception of the dan tian, each point has both a right and left location on the body.

The pattern of strikes originates at the dantian, a point below the navel and considered the cradle of one's intrinsic energy, travels along the soft tissue and muscles of the extremities, and returns back to the dantian in the same manner that the circulation of breath follows. After approximately a year of consistent practice, the ridge hand strikes transition to fists as the practitioner grows accustomed to the conditioning. The density of fists provides a greater intensity to the strikes, thereby increasing the individual's tolerance levels to the contact.

At this stage, in addition to post-training massages, the practitioner typically also applies herbal liniments for a variety of purposes that range from toughening the skin to promoting circulation to healing injuries.

In advanced stages of paai da gung, the practitioner is trained to instinctively repel and counter while being struck. A transition to apparatus-oriented striking methods using bundled sticks, sand bags, and eventually sacks filled with smooth river stones is incorporated into the routines. Initially, bundled sticks are used by the individual to self-inflict strikes according to personal sensitivity levels. As progress is achieved, a partner will strike those points with announcements to alert the practitioner in the beginning and eventually move toward non-verbal hits to stimulate a reflexive repulsing response from the practitioner. At first, this is a static exercise. Ultimately, it is a dynamic conditioning sequence trained with stepping movements and shadow-boxing techniques.

When paai da gung is improperly or overly trained, the long-term damage can negate the short-term gains. Firstly, it cannot be practiced haphazardly or inconsistently. Consistency, patience, and the proper guidance are the keys to success in this area of martial training. Secondly, this practice cannot be viewed in isolation or as an ultimate end. In other words, paai da gung, if trained, is only a small part of the bigger picture of one's martial journey. Its intention was to prepare one for combat as a conditioning method in conjunction with efficient fighting techniques. It was not meant to be showcased as a skill in itself that would take the place one's actual fighting ability. One who may be impervious to blows is not the same as another who understands how evade and effectively execute them. Finally, mishaps from improper paai da gung training are permanent. Nerve damage, internal injury, mental instability, and in severe cases, death, are consequences of incorrect practice. While this training method has appealing qualities, its risky outcomes cannot be overlooked.

These set of extreme and obscure practices are methods that have been trained in many Chinese martial lineages, particularly during periods of intense conflict and warfare. In such times, intense conflict warranted intense training to raise spirits and to rally support. Survival, by any means, was encouraged over safety and precaution. Modern technologies and sports science, on the other hand, have explored the inherent flaws that can lead to long-term harm from such demanding training. Through this enlightenment to the hidden dangers of these established practices, it would be trivial to forfeit long-term wellness simply to mechanically carry out traditional training methods in today's times.

Yung Faat: Applications

A comprehensive understanding of techniques is acquired through direct experiences with their applications. *Yung faat* (用法), or usage, is the aspect of training that reinforces principles through diligent practice and lively execution. In Pak Mei, techniques are rehearsed on the muk yan jong and applications are trained through deui chaak kyun and san sau.

Muk yan jong (木人樁) – literally wooden person post; more commonly known as the wooden dummy, is a training apparatus used by many Chinese martial arts. The general construction of the muk yan jong consists of wooden appendages that act as arms and legs and a solid trunk that serves as the focus of close and extreme range strikes. Wooden dummy designs differ from school to school, depending on the training emphasis or the school's specific aims. Traditionally, the Pak Mei muk yan jong has two unique features that differentiate it from others. The first is a wooden simulation of a person's head that is fitted at the top of the training apparatus. This wooden replica enables the practitioner to focus on attacks to the head as well as to the trunk and extremities of the muk yan jong. The second specialized feature is the use of spring mechanisms in its construction. The entire muk yan jong rests on an oversized coil or a set of large springs to facilitate the use of ging within techniques. Pak Mei is a system based upon a comprehensive achievement of ging. It is believed that the solid and rigid structure of a standard wooden dummy may actually hamper issuing force, and in turn, encourage the use of lik, or muscular strength. By enlivening the muk yan jong with a pliable base, the practitioner is able to train techniques in a manner consistent with Pak Mei principles. In most cases, the wooden head is also supported by a large coil to reproduce head movement and neck behaviors.

As a practitioner becomes proficient with the intricacies of Pak Mei techniques, partnered practice becomes essential. To assist in interactive training, *deui chaak kyun* (對拆拳) – literally paired tearing form; better known as a two-person set, is practiced. Deui chaak kyun merges the techniques from forms training with the practical applications for each movement. In the two-person routine, each individual is responsible for a prearranged set of techniques. While the principles of simultaneous attack and defense are inherent in each technique, each individual must assume the mindset of being offensive or defensive throughout the form. This critical component enables the practitioners to experience and understand the execution of techniques in a controlled setting. Essential elements of combat such as timing, accuracy, range, sensing, and technique are all trained in a comprehensible and reproducible manner in the two-person set. The Pak Mei system has multiple two-person sets, and in many lineages, two-person weapons routines exist as well, particularly *deui chaak gwan* (對拆棍), or the two-person staff.

After practitioners accumulate experience and gain confidence from deui chaak kyun, they proceed to *saan sau* (散手) – free sparring; literally dispersing hands. Saan sau tests the practitioners' abilities in a less predictable manner than in deui chaak kyun. At this stage, practitioners freely *disperse* the techniques that they have been taught. While conventional strikes such as punches and kicks are trained, crucial factors such as distance, angles and timing are learned. Adept practitioners will become accustomed to distances, deflecting and redirecting in the close range and naturally move onto trapping and locking in the extreme range. Traditionally, saan sau was practiced bare-chested and bare-knuckled, many times with the victor towering over his defeated, and in some cases unconscious, opponent. Under the careful supervision of a competent teacher, practitioners can develop a thorough understanding of the dynamics of attack and defense, and respond effectively.

CHAPTER SIX

Kyun

"All fixed set patterns are incapable of adaptability or pliability. The truth is outside of all fixed patterns."

- Bruce Lee

(1940 – 1973)

Kyun (拳), or forms, are formalized routines that pass on the primary principles and key techniques from a teacher to a student of a particular martial art. According to conventional understanding, there are four core forms that embody the martial methodology of unadulterated Pak Mei Kung Fu. Theoretically, these four forms convey the true essence of what would be considered the standards and skills of Pak Mei Kung Fu.

With regard to the actual number of forms that are considered to have a purely Pak Mei influence, it should be noted that Master Cheung Lai Chuen had the propensity to furnish different individuals with different knowledge. These inconsistencies pertaining to the number of key forms that represent authentic Pak Mei methods often fluctuated between three and four. What is consistent is that the origins of the imported forms from Lau Man Paai, Lei Ga and Lung Ying are clearly made known. Furthermore, each genealogy stemming from Cheung Lai Chuen may have either an abridged or an extended program due to each individual's respective experiences or personal adaptations that were made to the teaching curriculum.

In this section, all forms will be discussed beginning with the core Pak Mei forms.

Jik Bou Kyun: Straight Stepping Form

Regarded as the foundational form, *Jik Bou Kyun* (直步拳), or Straight Stepping Form, is the first set to be trained among the routines that are considered indigenous and authentic Pak Mei forms. Jik Bou trains the practitioner to coordinate luk ging with sei noi biu ging to energize and direct the form's straightforward techniques in a highly developed manner.

Pertaining to luk ging – the six sectors of kinetic bridging, Jik Bou directs the practitioner to stabilize the stance in order to properly root the practitioner's foundation. This in turn enables the issuing force to be drawn up from the legs, spiraled through the waist and torso, and released through the extremities. Sei noi biu ging – the 4 dynamic and directional forces, actively harmonizes the phases of martial force and provides the route in which the issuing force should travel: inward, outward, upward, or downward. Throughout this entire process, the internal focus is linking to and leading the external expression. The deceptive simplicity of the

124

techniques actually conceals the subtle complexities inherent in the form. In terms of mobility, the footwork trains the novice to charge forward to close the distance between practitioner and opponent.

A number of versions of Jik Bou exist to date as a result of Master Cheung Lai Chuen's differentiated instruction and further differentiation of the form stemming from the generations of successive instructors from his lineage. Trademark techniques that characterize Jik Bou regardless of degrees of differentiation are *biu ji* (鏢指; shooting fingers) and *chyun sam fung ngaan cheui* (穿心鳳眼搥; penetrating the heart phoenix-eye punch). While variations may be practiced, Jik Bou fundamentally emphasizes fully integrated body movement in coordination with specific breathing patterns to enhance the issuing force of the form's techniques.

Gau Bou Teui: Nine Step Push

The second form considered an authentic Pak Mei form, *Gau Bou Teui* (九步推), or Nine Step Push, refines the foundations of Jik Bou to further develop the practitioner's ging, or force manifestation. Gau Bou Teui is a transformative form that is dependent upon the skillful coordination of luk ging and sei noi biu ging. While Jik Bou trains the proper mechanics of techniques, Gau Bou Teui emphasizes the execution and expansion of those techniques.

The focus of Gau Bou Teui is centered on the continuous application of techniques using issuing force rather than sheer strength. Jik Bou provides a firm foundation through a repetitive series of techniques designed to facilitate efficient qi flow thereby energizing the internal organs and extremities to optimize performance. This essentially trains the practitioner to rely less upon inherent muscular strength and more upon intrinsic force production. Gau Bou Teui requires this foundation to be in place in order to amplify the range of what has already been established by Jik Bou, and to further instruct the practitioner to channel the body's unified force through the extremities in a steady and acute manner. Pressuring footwork and directed hand skills are intended to penetrate an opponent's defenses and instantaneously attack vital targets along the body within a close range – which is usually an unfamiliar and uncomfortable distance for many opponents.

While there are numerous descriptions attempting to explain the significance of Nine Step Push, the fundamental impression of the form is that it is an extension of Jik Bou. Some plausible explanations for the title include: from an aerial view, the pattern of the form is in the shape of the character nine, or 九; there are a series of nine steps linked with hand techniques leading to the push that is repeated three times within the form; there is a combination of nine reinforcing or alternating hand skills such as *seung teui jeung* (雙推掌; double pushing palms) or *chyun mo* (穿摩; penetrating stripping [hand]), respectively. Despite the range of reasons, specialized techniques such as *lo hon tyut sa ga* (羅漢脫裟伽; the Buddhist monk [Lohan] removes his cassock) epitomize the sophisticated hand skills found in Gau Bou Teui.

Sap Baat Mo Kiu: 18 Stripping Bridges

Sap Baat Mo Kiu (十八摩橋), or Eighteen Stripping Bridges, is considered the third authentic Pak Mei form in the system. When the practitioner has reached a level of proficiency in Jik Bou and Gau Bou Teui, this form trains the practitioner to simultaneously suppress and attack upon sensing the opponent's bridges. At this stage, the practitioner's skill level is highly developed and extremely efficient; hence, the techniques need to match the practitioner's capability, respectively. The essence of this form develops the practitioner's fighting fluidity and flexibility – the skill of changing and chaining attacks to suppress and smother an opponent.

Sap Baat Mo Kiu takes advantage of the close range to disrupt the opponent's comfort zone and to penetrate the vital cavities on the opponent's body. The principles and techniques in this form were formulated in response to opponents who favored longer fighting distances. The short distance enabled the practitioner to: jam any attacks that needed a big wind-up; entangle – or strip, the opponent's arms to create optimal entry points; and, puncture the opponent's visceral zones. To get within range, the practitioner presses forward with *bik bou* (逼步), or the pressing step. This drives the stealthy hand techniques into a position that disables the opponent's capacity to effectively attack with the extremities.

Within certain lineages, Sap Baat Mo Kiu is better known as *Sap Baat Mo Gwai Sau* (十八魔鬼手), or Eighteen Evil Ghost Hands, to denote the destructive nature of the techniques housed within this form. Sap Baat Mo Gwai Sau instructs the practitioner to dissolve an opponent's incoming force, stifle all attacks, and pierce through the opponent's defenses using 18 particular dynamic hand methods. The term ghost hands refers to the undetectable and incalculable nature of the techniques. The evil aspect of these methods represents the vital targets that are attacked on the opponent's body. For this form to be truly effective, the five skills need to be mastered: heavy hands, sticking hands, stealing hands, shock force, and poison hands. Without these attributes, the techniques are merely hollow movements. It is for this reason that this is an advanced form.

Since different lineages in all likelihood may have distinct terms for techniques or methods, listing the eighteen hand methods may raise more concerns rather than serve to enlighten. The 18 bridges regardless of technique names ideally adapt to whatever shifts or changes occur within an altercation. As a cohesive collection of infiltrating concepts and methods, they provide the practitioner with an array of options that blend together into a seamless stream of stripping and striking attacks. While the standard of Sap Baat Mo Kiu or Sap Baat Mo Gwai Sau rests with each practitioner's own exposure to the form, techniques such as *seung taan kiu* (雙彈橋; double flicking bridges), *mo kiu fu jaau* (摩橋虎爪; stripping bridge / tiger claw), and *jong cheui* (撞搥; colliding strike) are unique to this form regardless of differentiation among various Pak Mei genealogies.

Maang Fu Cheut Lam – Fierce Tiger Comes Out of the Forest

Maang Fu Cheut Lam (猛虎出林), or Fierce Tiger Comes Out of the Forest, is considered the highest form in Pak Mei Kung Fu. At this stage in the practitioner's training, the qi and its efficacy are highly developed, enabling all body parts to become energized and operational in an optimized capacity. As such, the techniques are highly aggressive, devised specifically to uproot and displace while simultaneously seeking to disarm, disfigure, and ultimately disembowel the enemy.

Maang Fu Cheut Lam emphasizes the use of the fu jaau and the tearing and ripping applications that accompany the tiger claw formation. Supple joints, such as the wrists in particular, accommodate quick changes in response to an opponent's reactions. The sinuous movements facilitate the smooth transfer of qi, instantaneously energizing the hands to form and strengthen the force of the fu jaau. In application, the grabs adhere to the opponent's body parts, prevent further attacks, and in the same instant, tear into soft tissues and sensitive nerve sites. While essentially all of the hand formations are employed in Gau Bou Teui and Sap Baat Mo Kiu, the tiger claw is almost exclusively applied in Maang Fu Cheut Lam. This demonstrates the destructive and determined nature of this form.

The name Maang Fu Cheut Lam is a unique designation that departs from the naming conventions of the prior three forms. Jik Bou, Gau Bou Teui, and Sap Baat Mo Kiu all include a specific footwork term or hand maneuver expression such as bou (step), teui (push), or mo kiu (stripping bridge). Maang Fu Cheut Lam, on the other hand, emphasizes the spirit of a tiger leaving the comforts of its forest habitat to hunt and slaughter its prey. Although this vicious metaphor is meant to express the attitude and position that the practitioner should maintain toward an enemy, it may also convey a clue to its origin.

In some lineages, it is noted that this form was created by Master Cheung Lai Chuen himself to bring the style to the next level using the authentic Pak Mei material that he was taught. Upon further examination, the term *maang fu* set within a contemporary context means *fearless fighter*. From this perspective, Cheung Lai Chuen is the fearless fighter who, in essence, left the confines of his hometown *Huiyang* (惠陽; *Waiyeung* in Cantonese) to become the fearless freedom fighter of Donggong, bringing his martial art out into the urban atmospheres of Southern China during the early to middle portions of the 20th Century. The name of the form may have been modified to cunningly honor the great master, particularly since within some earlier lineages, Maang Fu Cheut Lam was known simply as *Fu Bou* (虎步), or Tiger Step.

Despite speculation pertaining to its origin, Maang Fu Cheut Lam is the system's highest form. The intensity of *ji lik* (指力), or finger strength, is the key to an effective fu jaau; and, the mastery of qigong is the source of powerful ji lik. At the summit of the practitioner's training, these specialized attributes contribute to techniques such as *lip sau* (獵手; hunting hand) and *waan sau fu jaau* (挽手虎爪; pulling hand / tiger claw) that are specific to Maang Fu Cheut Lam. In modern martial terms, the concepts and techniques of this form fall under the category of clinch fighting or dirty boxing – a phase of combat that is unavoidable in close-range fighting.

Ultimately, whether it was a preexisting form or one masterfully organized and crafted by Master Cheung Lai Chuen, Maang Fu Cheut Lam is an advanced set that requires more than the internalization of the previous three original forms in combination with a specialized set of skills. Maang Fu Cheut Lam requires the practitioner to uphold the highest degree of control and restraint before releasing the fierce tiger from the forest.

Sap Ji Ying Jaau Kau Da Kyun: Ten Character Eagle Claw Holding Striking Form

Sap Ji Ying Jaau Kau Da Kyun (十字鷹爪扣打拳), or literally [In the outline of the Chinese] Ten Character Eagle Claw Holding Striking Form, is typically the first form that is taught to the beginner after Jik Bou due to the directness of many of the techniques within this form. Originally from *Lau Man Paai* (流民派), or the Wanderers' style, Sap Ji – as it is better known, was taught to Cheung Lai Chuen from his first teacher, Lam Sek (林石).

Lau Man Paai was typically known as a vagrant or beggar art that emphasized very direct and crude methods that were extremely effective, particularly for the streets. Hence, in Sap Ji, simultaneous grabbing and striking, a variety of elbows and stealthy kicks are trained. The stances are stable and the footwork is mobile, enabling the practitioner to move in a very realistic and practical martial manner.

The number of movements in this form varies greatly between different lineages. Some Hong Kong versions, compared to earlier versions of Sap Ji from Guangdong, are typically shortened by approximately 15 opening movements. In some lineages there is *Siu Sap Ji* (小十字; Small Ten Character) and *Daai Sap Ji* (大十字; Big Ten Character) to facilitate the teaching curriculum. Ying jaau, *dai paang jin chi* (大鵬展翅; big bird spreads its wings), and *bui cheui* (背搥; back punch) are distinguishing techniques that are found in this form.

It should be noted that this was the only form that Cheung Lai Chuen allowed to be publicly demonstrated by Pak Mei practitioners while he was alive.

Saam Mun Kyun: Three Doors Form

Saam Mun Kyun (三門拳), or three doors form, is a combative set that originated from *Lei Ga* (李家) – the fighting methods of the Lei Family, more commonly spelled and established in the Mandarin form as Li. While Li is a common Chinese surname with several distinct martial genealogies, the lineage under *Li Yi* (李義) taught to Cheung Lai Chuen by *Li Mung* (李曚) of the Donggong region is the lineage from which this form is derived. Saam Mun Kyun emphasizes attacks to the three doors, or mun, on the opponent's body.

Techniques from Li Ga typically cover both mid and short attacking ranges, which complement the close and extreme ranges of the principal Pak Mei sets. An array of arm locking and breaking techniques within the mid-range distance enables the practitioner to close the gap and strike the vital targets found in the opponent's upper, middle, or lower doors. The intricate footwork trains the practitioner to counterattack against multiple opponents using locks, trips and concealed kicks. Coupled with the calculated *kam na sau* (擒拿手; widely known in the Mandarin form as qinna) – seizing and capturing hands, the legs complete the controlling methods that are prevalent throughout this form.

Depending on the practitioner's lineage, Saam Mun Kyun is also known by *Saam Mun Baat Gwa Kyun* (三門八卦拳; Three Doors Eight Diagram Form) or *Saam Mun Cheui* (三門搥; Three Doors Striking), whereby the latter term is usually used by the later lineages and the former title has been preserved by Cheung Lai Chuen's earlier students. In some lineages, *chaap cheui* (插搥; piercing punch) is a midrange strike directed at the middle door while *haap kiu* (挾橋; holding the bridge [under the arm]) is an arm lock that can quickly convert to an arm break when combined with the proper footwork. Distinguishing techniques such as these in combination with methods from Sap Ji provide the practitioner with a formidable fundamental fighting foundation.

Dei Saat Kyun: Ground Killing Form

Dei Saat Kyun (地殺拳), or Ground Killing Form, is a ground fighting set that was adopted from Li Ga. The emphasis on using the legs as the primary attacking approach makes this an exceptionally distinct form from all the others within the Pak Mei system. By using the legs, the practitioner's fighting range is extended, enabling the practitioner to add long range to the preexisting mid and close ranges that are covered by the techniques from the other forms.

The sophisticated footwork found in this form trains the practitioner to attack opponents from a longer distance, disable stances, and to take opponents to the ground. *Seung daan geuk* (雙彈腳), or double flicking kick, targets an opponent's lower extremities and groin. The force and range covered by this kick is much stronger and longer than the strength and reach of the arms working from the same distance. *Gaap geuk* (夾腳), or clipping leg, locks the opponent's foot while tightening the rest of the leg. This maneuver is meant to dislocate and immobilize the opponent's legs. *Jin geuk* (剪腳), or scissor legs, is designed to take down an opponent. This technique requires timing, accuracy and the appropriate distance for it to be effective. As with all kicking techniques and leg methods, sound judgment coupled with extensive training need to be in place before such techniques are considered for actual use.

Sei Mun Baat Gwa Kyun: Four Doors Eight Diagram Form

In an effort to bridge the foundational fighting forms with the core Pak Mei sets, Cheung Lai Chuen created Sei Mun Baat Gwa Kyun (四門八卦拳). The Four Doors Eight Diagram Form, as it is literally translated, is a fusion of the techniques that the great master considered most important and most effective from all of the martial methods that he had learned prior to his indoctrination into Pak Mei principles and techniques.

The term mun in a broader martial sense, apart from meaning door or gate, refers to a martial system. The gate relates to the entrance or archway that an individual must walk under to enter a *mou gun* (武館), or training hall. The signboard above the entrance indicates which mun, or gate, that one will be entering. The sei mun in this respect refers to the four styles that Master Cheung Lai Chuen honored: Lau Man Paai, Li Ga, Lung Ying, and Ngo Mei Siu Lam. The Hakka heritage of these four styles typically placed emphasis on practicality and stealth for sheer survival. Hence, the crux of this form relies upon those same key qualities to overwhelm and overcome multiple attackers.

Combatively, this comprehensive form attempts to cover the sei mun, or four personal directions – front, right, back, and left, and the baat gwa, or the eight compass directions – north, northeast, east, southeast, south, southwest, west, and northwest. Essentially, the practitioner is defending the sei mun, while executing multidirectional attacks within the range of the baat gwa.

The techniques found in Sei Mun Baat Gwa Kyun address all distances as well as multiple adversaries. A strong emphasis on kicks is prevalent throughout this form to deal with numerous opponents. Chyun sam geuk and *fu mei geuk* (虎尾腳; tiger tail kick) attack opponents to the practitioner's front and rear, respectively. With regard to hand techniques, chaap cheui, bui cheui, and *seung kau sau* (雙扣手; double grasping hands) cover the mid and close ranges to effectively take advantage of the distance that has been closed by the kicks. As the footwork both closes and opens opportunities, the hands also respectively shut down attacks and expose the opponent's entry points.

Ying Jaau Nim Kiu: Eagle Claw Sticking Bridge

Ying Jaau Nim Kiu (鷹爪黏橋), or Eagle Claw Sticking Bridge, is an advanced level form imported from Lung Ying Kyun – Dragon Style Kung Fu. Within Lung Ying Kyun, the techniques from this form are synonymous with the methods found in *Lung Ying Mo Kiu* (龍形摩橋), or Dragon Shape Sensing Bridge, an essential form of the Dragon system. This is a highly aggressive form which trains the practitioner to adhere to and smother the opponent. The main goals are to stick to the opponent's extremities, control the opponent's actions, and to overwhelm the opponent's spirit and physical capacity.

The techniques in Ying Jaau Nim Kiu are executed within close and extreme ranges against opponents. Extensive bridge engagement emphasizes sticking to the arms which leads to adhering to the body – this ideally suppresses the opponent's ability to execute techniques efficiently. Within the same vein, *kau pek* (扣劈; grasping chop) and *seui kiu* (碎橋; smashing bridge) are specific techniques that disable the opponent's arms, creating seamless opportunities to attack vital cavities on the body. Pressing footwork in the form of bik bou jams the opponent's lower extremities, further hampering the opponent's ability use the legs to counter. By training the methods found in Ying Jaau Nim Kiu, the practitioner learns to embrace the benefits of close range combat.

It is important to note that while Ying Jaau Nim Kiu and Lung Ying Mo Kiu are often used interchangeably within Pak Mei Kung Fu, they are not identical to the corresponding form in Lung Ying Kyun. Many of the technical names, the arrangement of techniques, and the applications for the techniques differ in each form with respect to each other's martial art. Regardless of semantics, at advanced levels, sticking and sensing skills work as one to dynamically engage bridges in order to prevail over opponents.

Ng Hang Mo: Five Element Stripping

Perhaps no other set within the Pak Mei system can create as much controversy as the mere mention of Ng Hang Mo (五行摩), or Five Element Stripping. Considered one of the most advanced sets in the system to some, yet regarded as nonexistent by others, this routine has eluded many modern day practitioners.

An exclusive cluster of Cheung Lai Chuen's inner-chamber disciples had received instruction in the principles of this routine. It is certain that the master's two sons, Cheung Bing Sum and Cheung Bing Fat, learned the key concepts of the set. Therefore, the branches stemming from these inner-chamber disciples have had access to this specialized training set. Whether it has been preserved or even transmitted within these branches depended upon the willingness of the teacher to pass on the knowledge and teachings to successive students. The more reserved the teacher, the lesser the likelihood of the transmission of this training routine.

The lesser acquainted the instructor, the greater the potential for the denial of its existence.

With reverence for *mou dak* (武德; martial morality) within the Pak Mei martial clan, no more shall be said about this set except for the fact that it is what it is – a routine devised to train a specific skill rather than any specific techniques. In the same manner that body parts are conditioned and the skill of striking meridians and body cavities is acquired – and are not considered kyun, or forms, Ng Hang Mo trains a specific ability to nullify an adversary's pressing assault by employing the theory of the five phases, or elements: *muk* (木; wood), *fo* (火; fire), *tou* (土; earth), *gam* (金; metal), and *seui* (水; water). Five directional footwork patterns in combination with five interchangeable attacking hand methods within the context of the five elements form the basis of this routine.

While some teachers have made claims that this is an incomplete set, the reality of the situation is that the material requires an extensive amount of keenness and reflection to understand and an even greater amount of time devoted to the practice of these phases, or elements.

Bing Hei: Weaponry

Bing hei (兵器), or weaponry, is an integral part of any martial art's training curriculum. Within traditional Chinese martial arts, weapons represent a link to the past in addition to being tools that teach a specific martial skill. During the dynastic periods in China, weapons such as the butterfly swords, tiger fork, double broadswords, and the like were used by individuals to defend themselves against invasions or employed by invaders to attack the masses. However, in the modern context, these same armaments are obsolete and unrealistically wielded. Still, while sticks and swords have been replaced by guns and knives, the importance of understanding weapons and their function remains vital in formulating a comprehensive understanding of martial principles.

Within Pak Mei Kung Fu, weapons are viewed as extensions of an individual's ability to manifest force from a fully integrated body both into and throughout an object, in this case a staff or sword. It is believed that if a practitioner cannot issue force properly, the weapon that is wielded by the practitioner will not be able to be used effectively. Weapons in this circumstance provide a means to challenge a practitioner to meet a martial standard and to raise the practitioner's level of training and experience.

On a general level, an individual learns the intricacies of how to effectively manipulate an apparatus in confrontational situations. A staff would be handled very differently from a pair of butterfly swords; and accordingly, a pair of butterfly swords would maneuver very differently from a straight sword. Experience with a variety of weapons enables the practitioner to learn to accentuate the attributes of each particular weapon. This teaches the individual to account for weight distribution, range, positioning, and power peaks in each specialized weapon to optimize its efficiency.

The collection of weaponry that is trained in Pak Mei Kung Fu has predominantly been imported from

Lau Man Paai and Li Ga. The Wanderers Sect was known to amass an assortment of weapons that ranged from established to uncommon armaments such as the double broadswords to the tiger fork, respectively. Li Ga, on the other hand, was renowned primarily for the clan's staff skills. While many practitioners have chosen to augment the system by supplementing the training curriculum with their own weapons experiences, a core set of key weapons were deemed worthwhile to the system by Cheung Lai Chuen.

Bladed Weapons: A Family of Swords

Under the category of weapons with cutting capacity, three distinct swords are emphasized in Pak Mei: the double butterfly swords, the double broadswords and the straight sword.

Jeui Wan Lau Yip Seung Dou (追魂柳葉雙刀), or Chasing Spirits Willow Leaf Double Swords, is the official name of the set employing the Southern-specific butterfly swords. With hand guards that are typically used to flip the swords to: block close range attacks, protect the forearms, and facilitate extreme-range cutting, the butterfly swords are used by many Southern-based Chinese martial arts. Each Southern family, style or system has its own unique method of using the butterfly swords; and, in some cases, more than one routine is trained in using the butterfly knives. Within Pak Mei, techniques such as *gwaat dou* (刮刀; scraping knives) and *fan dao* (分刀; dividing knives) characterize the manner in which the short swords are used. The forearm-length blades make this set of swords ideal for close range encounters, emulating the system's close range hand techniques.

Fei Fung Seung Dou (飛鳳雙刀), or Flying Phoenix Double Swords, is the double broadsword set in Pak Mei Kung Fu. While double broadsword techniques are found in both Southern and Northern systems, the martial applications from both regions typically exhibit a Northern influence. Since the wide stances and expansive movements in this form are not native to the close range principles found in Pak Mei, practitioners may find the movements to be quite a different martial challenge. Techniques such as *seung jaam dou* (雙斬刀; double beheading swords) and *seung cha dou* (雙叉刀; double intersecting swords) extend the attacking range to cover both mid and long range distances. A successful combination of multidirectional footwork and synchronized swordplay trains the practitioner to address and eradicate multiple attackers in a highly aggressive manner. Compared to the butterfly swords, the lengthy broadswords cover a wider range in both distance and cutting capacity.

Ching Lung Gim (青龍劍), or Green Dragon Straight Sword, is the system's double-edged sword form. The gim, like the double broadswords – also found in both Southern and Northern Kung Fu systems, is by and large a Northern-based sword. Furthermore, as with any weapon, its usage varies from style to system and even from individual to individual. The double-edged blade requires a degree of control and finesse that distinguishes its maneuverability from the previous two swords. In principle, the sword's direct strikes and diffusion of incoming attacks mirror the methods found in the system's hand techniques. The strength of the blade is dependent upon the practitioner's grip and wrist agility; the movement of the cutting edges reflects the practitioner's skill; and, the spirit of the sword is contingent upon the practitioner's intent and will. *Chi gim* (刺劍; stabbing straight sword) and *pek gim* (劈劍; splitting straight sword) are characteristic techniques that require the practitioner to have a mastery of body connection and weapon coordination in order to effectively execute such movements. The length of the straight sword – typically the span of a practitioner's vertically extended arm to the side's corresponding earlobe, provides midrange coverage. When combined with its offensive footwork, the range is broadened to contend with the longer distances between a practitioner and opponents.

Wooden Weapons: The Casual and Common Arsenal

Within this category, the bench and the pole were traditionally everyday objects that could be used for personal defense at a moment's notice. Their ordinary presence in pre-modern China made them easily accessible and unassuming as weapons.

Sin Fa Bou Dang (仙花寶凳), or Immortal Flower Treasure Bench, is a routine that was incorporated from one of Cheung Lai Chuen's earliest instructors, Lam Sek. The immediate and martially practical attributes of this apparatus enabled it to be viewed as an asset amongst the repertoire of Pak Mei weaponry. Expertise with a bench was particularly useful for travelers – or wanderers, who often found themselves in public situations such as inns or tea houses. *Paau dang* (拋凳; throwing bench) and *baai dang* (擺凳; swinging bench) are techniques that increase the range between the practitioner and opponents. All parts of the bench: legs, sides and seat, are used in combination with pressing footwork to ward off attackers or to strike sensitive zones.

Daai Jan Gwan (大陣棍), or Great Formation Pole, is one of two key staff forms that were imparted from the collection of martial methods from Li Ga. Cheung Lai Chuen maintained a close relationship with Li kinfolk under his apprenticeship with his teacher Lei (Li) Mung. As a result, he was accepted as part of the Li clan and was shown a wide array of weapons that were typically reserved for family members. Daai Jan Gwan is a pole set designed to combat multiple attackers. The techniques strike all levels of the saam mun: the opponent's upper, middle and lower doors. Both single end and double end pole techniques are executed in multiple directions at multiple angles. The techniques *saat gwan* (殺棍; killing pole) and *fu mei gwan* (虎尾棍; tiger tail pole) are single end strikes, while *jong gwan* (撞棍; colliding pole) requires the practitioner to shift the grip to the center of the staff to prepare for a series of strikes using both ends of the pole. In Daai Jan Gwan, the long range wards off adversaries, closes the distance, and primes the opponent for more significant and disabling strikes in the close range.

Ng Hang Jung Lan Gwan (五行中攔棍), or Five Element Central Guarding Pole, is the second staff set integrated within the Pak Mei system from Li Ga. The five elements refer to cycles of creation and destruction through the interaction of the five elements: wood, fire, earth, metal, and water. Each element represents a specific attribute that the pole assumes during a specific technique. *Paau gwan* (拋棍; throwing pole), *chyun sam gwan* (穿心棍; piercing the heart pole), *laam gwan* (攬棍; grasping pole), *fong gwan* (妨棍; obstructing pole), and *saat gwan* (殺棍; killing pole) are techniques that adhere to each respective element's characteristics. Unlike Daai Jan Gwan which emphasizes methods against multiple attackers, Ng Hang Jung Lan Gwan concentrates on technique theory and ging manifestation in the pole. Accordingly, this set solely trains single-ended pole maneuvers since the practitioner's skill level at the advanced stage enables force to be projected throughout the entire length of the pole at a very high level. Ideally, opponents can be overcome from the long range by the sheer precision of the techniques and the power exerted throughout the pole.

Unique Weapons: Unusual and Effective Training Tools

Under the category of unique weapons, the *daai pa* (大扒; literally: big hay fork; more commonly known as the tiger fork) and *seung gwaai* (雙柺; literally: an old man's walking cane; more commonly known as the crutches) are at the extremes in terms of size and execution. The daai pa is a long, three-pronged apparatus; the gwaai are slightly longer than the length of the forearms. The tiger fork can pierce and penetrate from a distance; the crutches club and ram in the mid and close ranges. Each weapon's attributes accentuate the distinctiveness of each apparatus.

144

The daai pa was actually divided into two classifications which were defined by its purpose as a farming implement and a tiger hunting tool. As a piece of farming equipment, the pa was used as a rake to assist in the maintenance and transport of the harvest or to aid in any oversized farming activities. The prongs of the fork were relatively close together – approximately a palm's width between each of the three prongs. The form derived from this setting is known as *Chin Ji Daai Pa* (千字大耙; Ten Thousand Character Big Fork). As a weapon used to combat tigers that wandered into villages in search of food, the pa was wielded by the tiger hunting sifu with his team of two young assistants. The prongs on this fork needed to be much further apart – approximately a forearm's length between each of the three thick prongs, in order to fend off an attacking tiger and to pierce the hide of the encroaching animal. The routine that trained the necessary techniques to handle this daunting task is called *Fo Dei Saam Cha Daai Pa* (火地三叉大扒; Fo Dei [an area in Sichuan Province] Three-Pronged Big Trident).

In the modern era, the tiger fork is passé on many levels, especially as a weapon to be used against multiple opponents. However, its versatility as both a training device and martial learning tool makes it an essential apparatus within the collection of weapons in Pak Mei. As a system that concentrates on the development and refinement of optimized force emission, Pak Mei training methods tend to avoid direct weight lifting activities. The bulk that can build from such exercises have a tendency to hinder the progress of ging – integrated force production, and further support the use of lik – muscular strength. This is often known as *sei lik* (死力), or dead strength, whereby muscular strength is not always as efficient in an active martial capacity. On the other hand, tiger fork techniques such as *sou pa* (掃扒; sweeping fork) and *laam pa* (攬扒; grasping fork), train ging and teach the practitioner to proficiently maneuver such a heavy weapon while being able to produce the force necessary to make the weapon martially effective. This active practice gives the routine a sense of martial purpose, which in turn, requires the practitioner to reflect upon the relationship between the practitioner and the weapon. Properties such as torsion and force dynamics, and skills such as functional control enable the weapon to be wielded in the most efficient manner. As an advanced level weapon, the daai pa provides a practitioner with the means and understanding to effectively maneuver long and heavy weapons on the whole.

Among the short weapons in Pak Mei, the gwaai are the most coveted and demanding in the system. While the gwaai is typically considered an assistive walking device such as a cane or crutch, its martial reference associates it more closely with the tonfa – the traditional Okinawan weapon that is also found in many other Asian martial arts. A perpendicular handle affixed to a cylindrical shaft running slightly past the length of the forearm, the gwaai are a pair of wooden implements with varying origins that seem to be based more upon fictitious folklore than fact. It is believed that the martial gwaai were weapons indigenous to the Hakka – more specifically, to the Wanderer's sect. From there, it was privately practiced and personally passed on solely within family members of the sect. In areas where weapons were illegal, the inconspicuous gwaai were obscure enough to pass for any woodworking implement and could be easily concealed within a jacket.

The means to effectively maneuver the gwaai originates in flexible yet firm wrists. In many respects, the gwaai is the most difficult weapon to master in Pak Mei. It is not the technical movements that pose a challenge to practitioners who are fortunate enough to receive instruction in this set of weapons, but rather, the ability to issue ging effectively through the gwaai. Since the wooden implements act as extensions of the arms, the body must be able to generate the force from the stance, channel it through the torso and extremities, and transfer it into the gwaai. The wrists are the hubs through which the force is regulated and given a directional vector in which the gwaai can go. In the routine *Wui Waan Seung Gwaai* (回環雙枴), or Circling Surrounding Double Crutches, techniques such as *paak gwaai* (拍枴; beating crutches) and *jong gwaai* (撞枴; colliding crutches) rely upon the wrists to effectively convey the necessary force to properly execute the techniques. The gwaai can be swiveled to attack the midrange by maximizing the momentum from the swing and directing the full force into a strike; or, the gwaai can be driven into the opponent's ribs in the extreme range with the butt ends of the weapons.

While there may be technical challenges in training this form, the bigger issue was commonly gaining access to this exclusive routine.

CHAPTER SEVEN

Ng Gung

"You must do the thing you think you cannot do."

- Eleanor Roosevelt,

Humanitarian (1884 – 1962)

Ng Gung (五功), or the Five Achievements, define martial mastery in Pak Mei. These skills: *chung sau* (重手; heavy hands), *nim sau* (黏手; sticking hands), *tau sau* (偷手; stealing hands), *ging jaak ging* (驚擲勁; startled tossing force / shock force), and *duk sau* (毒手; poison hands), authenticate the levels of combative expertise that an individual attains as an advanced Pak Mei practitioner. Certain skills can be acquired simultaneously; others require persistent effort and steady progress to approach an acceptable standard of proficiency according to traditional criteria. Ng Gung distinguishes the dedicated disciple from the casual student. While the Five Achievements may not represent every practitioner's pursuits, they exemplify the peaks of physical training and the summit of martial knowledge in Pak Mei. Each skill will be examined in this chapter.

Chung Sau: Heavy Hands

Chung sau is the term used to describe how hand techniques need to feel when they are applied. Heavy or weighted strikes give rise to sound and solid attacks. While the timing, distance, speed, and accuracy of a technique can all be flawlessly executed, the density of the strike intensifies the degree of damage. Under this notion, strikes are strengthened, and blocks themselves become strikes.

Heavy hands are developed through direct conditioning, fortified by formulaic breathing patterns, and reinforced through mental guidance. Sand bag training facilitates the physical aspect of priming the hands. Striking the bags along with the application of medicinal liniment familiarizes the practitioner with the actual sensation of hitting an object while toughening the surfaces around the hands. Qigong that is both inherent within the striking methods and supplemental to the physical training strengthens the hands and invigorates the strikes. As the qi reinforces each strike during training, it is programmed by the body to react in the same manner when actively engaged in combat. Standing qigong postures replenish the intrinsic energy to the hands by positively circulating the qi and preventing degenerative stagnation. These processes are initially led by the mind, which regulates intent, until all actions become involuntary. When this entire process becomes embedded within Pak Mei techniques, chung sau is realized.

The maintenance of heavy hands is an ongoing process. Traditionally, intense daily conditioning in combination with collaborative qigong methods lasted for a period of three continuous years. During this time, partnered exercises called *chai sau* (傑手), or detaining and hindering hands, make the hands *actively heavy*. The practitioner alternates between soft and hard – supple en route and sharp upon impact. These interactive exercises are the foundation for nearly all of the Five Skills in Pak Mei. The solo practice is almost useless without the functional application. Eventually, chai sau replaces the intense bag work, but not completely.

Chung sau is not merely the strength of the hands, but the manifestation of an integrated energetic connection between the mind and body. Initially, the mind must signal the body – the hands in particular, to act on an inanimate object, namely the sand bag. During chai sau, the mind directs the body to react in response to offensive stimuli provided by a live partner. When the mind, body and hands are synchronized and the signals between them are instinctive, chung sau is achieved.

Nim Sau: Sticking Hands

Nim sau refers to the skill of adhering to an opponent – not only to the arms, but more so to the body. This is not to be confused with the partnered routine known as *chi sau* (黐手), or sticking hands, made famous by Wing Chun (詠春) exponents. Sticking hands in this context is meant to smother an opponent's attacks in multiple dimensions, physically as well as psychologically.

Nim sau on a fundamental level focuses on the arms to adhere to and stifle strikes from an opponent. While an opponent customarily attacks with the extremities, those same bridges are also used for defense. Nim sau converts an opponent's offensive strikes to defensive checks by creating congestive conditions through unyielding contact. As a result, an opponent's preoccupation or frustration with a practitioner's unshakable extremities can shift the momentum of the attack to favor the practitioner's strategy.

Eight principles divided into defensive and offensive adhering applications govern nim sau skills. The defensive component of nim sau focuses upon intercepting an opponent's attacks. *Sip* (攝; absorb/dissipate) and *gang* (耕; cultivate) dissolve incoming forces while *fan* (分; separate/close) and *hyun* (圈; encircle) are evasive counters to an opponent's sticking maneuvers. The offensive aspect of nim sau concentrates on control and capture. *Chin* (纏; wrapping), *lak* (勒; entangling), *yik* (抑; restraining) and *laam* (攬; seizing) actively manipulate the opponent's bridges into submission. The defensive and offensive characteristics typically function in tandem, leading or reinforcing sticking hand applications. In addition, connections made with the opponent's bridges are based upon saam gwaan, or the three sections of the arm: the wrists, elbows, and shoulders.

On an advanced level, nim sau takes advantage of the opponent's spatial limitations and sticks to the opponent's vital targets rather than rely on the arms for containment. At this stage, the footwork primarily adheres to the opponent's movements, confining and pressuring the opponent in a *glutinous* manner. Targets typically housed within the visceral region are tenaciously and aggressively attacked, fortified by the influence of chung sau to ensure the penetration of each strike. Within the psychological realm, the overwhelming physical distractions are also designed to interfere with focus and concentration, creating further advantageous opportunities for the practitioner to exploit.

As with chung sau, the exercise that develops the capacity to effectively adhere to an opponent is chai sau. In the context of nim sau, chai sau refines the practitioner's ability to detect changes in an adversary's movement or intent. Since the arms can only move effectively within a certain range and will typically target vital areas, one can reasonably approximate the extent of all attacks that can be committed by the arms. Chai sau serves to eliminate this guesswork and to capitalize on competence by: enhancing the practitioner's ability to determine the direction by which an attack will come; teaching the practitioner to deflect incoming energy; and, training the practitioner to direct an attack toward a non-threatening angle. Practice with partners of varying ability, height, weight, physique, and intelligence is important to understanding how each or all factors influence the execution of effective nim sau.

Tau Sau: Stealing Hands

Stealing hands is the skill of exploiting the exposed and unguarded phases of an opponent's attacks. This differs from borrowing an opponent's strength, or *je lik* (借力), that is one of the cornerstone principles of *Taiji Quan Tui Shou* (太極拳推手; Great Extreme Boxing Push Hands; also known as Tai Chi Chuan Push Hands; pronounced *Taai Gik Kyun Teui Sau* in Cantonese). The concept of *sei leung po chin gan* (四兩破千斤), or four ounces repel one thousand catties, refers to using the opponent's own force to overcome himself in Taiji. In Pak Mei, tau sau actively deprives the opponent from attacking effectively while countering in the most opportune stage of the same attack.

The principle of yin and yang defines the skill of tau sau. Yin is passive, negative and insubstantial; yang is active, positive and substantial. Each technique is comprised of a cycle of yin and yang. Yin exists prior to a technique and subsequent to its execution while the commitment of the actual technique is yang. Tau sau detects the yin phase of an opponent's technique and aggressively steals the focus and force of the attack. Simultaneously, the practitioner presses the assault by stripping the opponent's balance and striking key areas that will create additional attacking opportunities. The steadfast search for the weaknesses, or yin phases, in techniques is the basis of stealing hands.

Advanced practitioners will use tau sau as a lure to ensnare opponents. At this level, yin and yang are already inherent in the practitioner's hand skills rather than merely found in the opponent's actions. Additionally, the practitioner's movements are instinctive and involuntary, which eliminates response lag. Those experienced in tau sau create the opportunities to expose the opponent's vulnerabilities rather than try to find the ideal instances.

Tau sau exhibits five fundamental features: sense, stick, stifle, steal and slay. *Mo* (摩), or sensing, at the mastery level is an instantaneous assessment of an opponent's overall capabilities. Nim, through techniques that cling to the extremities, ensures that the opponent is at a martial disadvantage. *Sak* (塞), to block or stifle, is the pivotal juncture of tau sau. At this phase, the practitioner proactively pursues weaknesses in the opponent's technique, structure or mindset to steal from – or tau. The completion of tau sau is finalized by *saat* (殺), or slaying. Alas, such finality was the psychology and nature of combat when Pak Mei Kung Fu was conceived.

Chai sau trained in this framework amplifies sensitivity levels and enhances response and reaction skills. As a partnered exercise, chai sau enables each practitioner to search and discover the yin phases of attacks in a controlled and observable atmosphere. After sensitivity, timing and range are improved, progress and proficiency in finding the flaws subsequently leads to learning to steal each other's advantage. As one learns to steal, the other is taught to guard. This simulation enables the practitioners to internalize the strategy and intuitively exhibit the skill.

Ging Jaak Ging: Startled / Shock Force

The highest personal achievement in Pak Mei is the attainment and execution of ging jaak ging – literally startled tossing force, or the martial manifestation of an individual's involuntary reaction to a shocking stimulus that has been refined and refitted to enhance the discharge of techniques. In other words, the opponent should feel physically jolted and wholly disjointed by a movement that has been delivered with ging jaak ging. Using the long-standing analogy of unknowingly being touched by the tip of a lit cigarette, ging jaak ging takes that shocking experience and applies it within a martial context. What has often been directly translated as scared power or shock force, ging jaak ging is the cultivation and modification of this startled reaction used to enhance a practitioner's issuing force against opponents. Within the spectrum of martial power, five particular classifications are used to differentiate between the degree of strength and quality of force that is applied when techniques are executed in Pak Mei. These categories are: *lik* (力), *baau faat lik* (爆發力), *ging* (勁), *faat ging* (發勁), and *ging jaak ging* (驚擲勁). While the differences may seem subtle, the implications are wide and vast.

Lik, or strength, is defined by muscular might. Actions employing lik rely solely on muscular strength and are limited to the individual's musculature and physique. Baau faat lik, or explosive issuing strength, also utilizes muscular strength in a more vigorous manner. In the same fashion that a sprinter uses an explosive thrust to leave the starting blocks of a 100 meter race, baau faat lik is exercised at the onset of techniques. Ging, or force, is the result of the harmonized effort of connective tissues and optimized qi working in unison to exert force. This method of performance is martially more efficient than the employment of lik or baau faat lik. Faat ging, or issuing force, is ging manifested in a dynamic manner. The lively execution of techniques is initiated by faat ging. This refined force is cultivated and utilized by many Chinese martial arts at advanced levels of practice due to its efficient and effective productivity.

Ging jaak ging is an integrated energetic detonation of martial force. Techniques are discharged in a sharp and sudden manner that is transferred directly to the core of the opponent. The acute level of this force is highly destructive. Ging jaak ging can be viewed as a live current compared to a car battery. It is highly volatile to both the opponent and the practitioner who is unable to recognize the detrimental aspects of this method of force delivery.

Training for ging jaak ging begins with learning global relaxation. Every inch of the body and every cell of the brain must acquire a sense of relaxation to optimize the flow of qi throughout the body. As the qi strengthens the internal organs, it is able to energize the extremities in the most efficient manner. When the energy is integrated through this synchronization, it can begin to be stored and emitted at will through the guidance of yi, or the intelligent mind.

Through the performance of the empty hand forms and the practice of chai sau, ging jaak ging can be safely nurtured and carefully developed. When a kyun, or hand form, is first learned, it is typically performed with lik because the mind is preoccupied with securing the movements. As the practitioner progresses, the physical expression of the form matures from using lik to employing ging. Since the expression conveys martial understandings, ging jaak ging can be trained to manifest itself within the practice of the forms. Over time, the expression of startled force is committed to muscle memory which facilitates the involuntarily employment of ging jaak ging during the execution of techniques at any moment. To assist interactively, chai sau is used here as well. Initially, the practitioners learn to transform the use of lik to ging with an actual person. Then, the practitioners progress to issuing and dissipating faat ging, the degree of force below ging jaak ging. Chai sau is performed at this level in order for the practitioners to experience the exertion of issuing force and to grasp the ability to avoid it within the safety of a more manageable ging. The energy exchanges between practitioners: alternate between supple and sharp as in training chung sau; adhere to each other as in the practice of nim sau; and, are stolen and guarded as in the interactions of tau sau. At the highest stage, chai sau incorporates the application of all four skills into one comprehensive exercise.

On the cautionary side regarding ging jaak ging, this particular skill can come at a rather high expense if trained improperly. The cultivation of startled force is very fire-based in terms of qigong metaphysics. This means that the training involved in attaining ging jaak ging stimulates a tremendous amount of hormone production – namely adrenalin and testosterone. Without the proper safety measures in place under the supervision of a qualified teacher, this hormonal excess can lead to major psychological and physical health issues such as psychosis or accelerated cellular degeneration in extreme cases. It is important to be aware of the side effects of this skill so that such debilitating ailments can be thwarted through preventative measures.

Duk Sau: Poison Hands

The previous four skills that were discussed could be individually and cooperatively attained through dedication and development over time. The fifth skill, duk sau, can only be passed directly from master to disciple. Poison hand skills, also known as dim mak, were traditionally only transferred to the heir of the system since the secrets needed to be safeguarded by an extremely upstanding individual with the highest degree of moral integrity, responsibility and reservation.

The prospect or method of transmission was left solely to the master's discretion. In many cases, the information was not passed to anyone. The absence of trustworthy students, the inflexible attitude of traditional teachers, or the premature demise of a master left many lineages devoid of this critical Kung Fu component. In the ideal scenario, a journal or manual was kept with this guarded information, in which case, the master's eldest son was typically bestowed the book and its contents. Unfortunately, particularly within the Southern regions of China, many teachers were illiterate. As a result, all of the information regarding poison hand skills was stored in their minds and was rarely disclosed unless the occasion required for it to be used. In other instances, particularly during warring periods, the teacher would reveal bits of duk sau information quite informally. It was then up to the astute student to record the details for future reference. For some teachers, amassing this indispensable information was through the chronicling of the parts and pieces that were infrequently imparted to them by their master.

One of the more commonly held beliefs is that poison hand knowledge is encoded within the empty hand routines. In some cases, it is believed that a series of fatal strikes are embedded within the sequence of techniques within a form. While this has been researched by many practitioners of various martial disciplines, due to the numerous variables that can interfere with the investigations, the results have predominantly been inconclusive. It is important, however, to note that the techniques within any form are designed to attack while defending, and the damage that can be caused by any strike has the potential to be lethal given the proper circumstances.

Authentic duk sau, on the other hand, is a methodical approach not only to seriously harm a person, but to remedy any trauma that the body has sustained. *Dit da* (跌打), literally fall-hit, is a term used to describe the treatment of injuries sustained from a fall or being hit. This skill was typically passed down through apprenticeship, as with the learning of kung fu. In fact, kung fu and dit da were typically taught together – both used for fortification and defense. Dit da experts treat bruises, bone brakes and internal injuries, but typically not illnesses. The use of liniments, poultices, plasters, patches and pills facilitate prevention as well as provide intervention. As previously mentioned on conditioning, dit da chou is used to preserve dexterity in the hands and to prevent rheumatoid arthritis. On the other hand, *dit da jau* (跌打酒) is used to remedy bruises by dispersing hematomas and promoting circulation. While some herbal formulas are specific to a particular martial lineage, others are family-kept secrets. Within Pak Mei, a myriad of recipes exist for all forms of dit da: a handful handed down from Cheung Lai Chuen; a larger collection passed down from the kin of Pak Mei practitioners.

Despite the technological and medical advances that are occurring everyday, dit da traditions continue to remain as effective today as they did in the past. While duk sau skills were intended to be destructive, dit da skills are very much constructive. In the immortal words of Pak Mei exponent and distinguished dit da practitioner of New York City's Chinatown, Chan Jim, "Taking a life is easy; saving one is difficult."

New York Pak Mei Kung Fu
Cultural Preservation Association

CHAPTER EIGHT

Anecdotes

"Every man is bound to leave a story better than he found it."

- Mary Augusta Ward,

Author (1851 – 1920)

In Chinese martial arts, stories over *yam cha* (飲茶), literally to drink tea, are meant to inform, inspire and establish a record of significant events within a particular style or system. However, the frequent embellishments with each telling and the exaggerations by each successive generation often tend to turn tales of successful achievements to incredulous exploits.

Within Pak Mei, the stories begin with Cheung Lai Chuen – the secular progenitor of Pak Mei Kung Fu. Cheung Lai Chuen was an individual shaped by his environment and driven by his circumstances. He was a formidable fighter, first and foremost – in essence, he fought to live and lived to fight. The stories recounted in this chapter are as they were told by Cheung Lai Chuen to Kwong Man Fong, or as experienced by Kwong Man

Fong with his master Cheung Lai Chuen. These anecdotes provide insights into the state of affairs in which these individuals lived and the situations which necessitated the enforcement of exceptional martial skills – and in many instances, extreme luck.

The Tiger Hunter's Apprentice

When Cheung Lai Chuen was twelve years old, it was around the turn of the 20th Century. Within his rural hometown of Huiyang, not much had changed since the previous century. Nature and the environment still dictated the lives of its inhabitants in this region.

By this time, Cheung had already learned Lau Man Paai and Li Ga, and he showed much promise in each art. His talent and abilities captured the attention of the village's tiger hunting sifu who happened to be looking for an apprentice. Tiger bones were used for medicinal purposes and were therefore highly valued. This teacher had already established a reputation with over fifty tiger kills with his *seung tit gon* (雙鐵桿) – double iron sticks. Since he was a member of the Wanderer's Sect thereby making him related to Lam Sek, Cheung's first teacher, the tiger hunting sifu decided to accept and train Cheung in the ways of tiger hunting. This did not mean that Cheung would no longer train his foundational martial methods; on the contrary, due to his competence, he could quickly learn the intricacies of tiger hunting. It was a rather normal occurrence for a teacher's training kin to train the same student in areas that would mutually benefit all of the individuals. Cheung Lai Chuen trained with the hunter daily, learning not only effective techniques but the vital targets to strike on the tiger.

On one particular day, the hunter learned that a tiger was spotted on the hillside by the village. The tiger hunting sifu quickly took Cheung Lai Chuen with him to witness how a tiger could be properly killed. He told the emerging teenager to climb up a tree to watch how he could easily slay the tiger. The hunter lured the tiger to a prearranged area. He raised his pair of gon as the tiger approached and began to circle around him. The sifu was supposed to strike the tiger on the nose with a series of fatal follow-up movements to finish it off. However, the sifu missed, striking the large animal under its eye. The iron rod, due to its age or lack of integrity, cracked in half. The hunter immediately struck the tiger in the face with the other gon, again missing the animal's nose. The tiger, enraged by the attacks, lunged at the sifu and decapitated him by sinking its teeth into the hunter's neck and tearing his head from his body. Cheung Lai Chuen was petrified and could not move as he witnessed the tiger behead his teacher. The tiger did not eat the tiger hunting sifu, and did not go after Cheung Lai Chuen who remained in the tree paralyzed with fear.

The death of his master severely traumatized him. After this incident, Cheung Lai Chuen decided that he did not want to assume the profession of a tiger hunter.

The Big Hunt for the Little Tiger

An 18 year-old Cheung Lai Chuen was called sifu by many of the residents of *Huizhou* (惠州; *Waijau* in Cantonese). Even though he personally felt that he was not quite qualified to assume the title sifu, Cheung taught some fundamentals of Lau Man Paai and Li Ga to a few boys in the neighborhood. This was the period before he received instruction in Pak Mei Kung Fu.

During this point in time, Huizhou was terrorized by a tiger that had descended the plateau in search of food. Chickens, pigs and other farm animals were being slaughtered by the tiger. Since Cheung Lai Chuen was considered the sifu of the vicinity, the natives appealed to him to get rid of the tiger. Witnesses said that the tiger was only about 100 pounds. Confident that he could easily take care of a 100 pound tiger cub, Cheung Lai Chuen enlisted the help of two of his students. Armed with a tiger fork, Cheung Lai Chuen was accompanied by two teenage students who were each equipped with a *tang dip* (藤碟), rattan shield, and broadsword. This was one typical structure of a tiger hunting team. At other times, one apprentice may use a rattan shield and broadsword while the other would use a rattan shield and a *long nga paang* (狼牙棒), wolf's tooth mace – essentially an elongated mace that rests on top of a club. The wolf's tooth mace would be used to distract and pry open the tiger's mouth while the person with the broadsword or master with the tiger fork would pierce and stab the tiger.

When the trio began to track the tiger, they witnessed that the paw print was enormous, suggesting that the tiger weighed much more than 100 pounds, and probably closer to the 200 pound range. By the time that they realized this, the tiger was closing in on the group of tiger hunters. The three individuals devised a quick strategy and ideally positioned themselves to deal with the imminent danger. One of Cheung's students rolled toward the tiger with the rattan shield and tried to come up from underneath to stab the tiger's throat. He missed and the tiger pounced on the student's shield, injuring the student's shoulder. The trapped student screamed out to Cheung Lai Chuen, "Help me, sifu!!" The other student circled around to try to get a better position.

Cheung Lai Chuen quickly charged to aid his student. He speared his tiger fork at the tiger, striking the tiger in the shoulder. This angered the tiger, causing it to react with a reflexive paw swat, hurling the tiger fork about 30 feet away from Cheung Lai Chuen, at the same knocking Cheung unconscious as he rolled down a hill from the force of the strike.

When he regained consciousness from the screams of his students, Cheung Lai Chuen quickly grabbed the tiger fork. The moment the tiger saw this movement, it began to charge toward Cheung Lai Chuen. Cheung thrust the fork upward into the attacking tiger's throat. This maimed the tiger and follow-up jabs killed it. He became the hero of Huizhou following this incident.

The Worst Possible Day

On the path to establishing a name for himself in *mou lam* (武林) – literally martial forest; symbolically the community of kung fu practitioners, in Guangzhou, Cheung Lai Chuen challenged many martial artists and accepted many challenges. After defeating a very powerful opponent named Chan Sau who had earned the title: The Champion of Five Counties, Cheung Lai Chuen consolidated his own reputation with his newly acquired status to become the Champion of Seven Counties. This became the envy of some and the source of anger for many of Chan Sau's followers. Chan had already amassed students who had students with students of their own, many of whom were learning martial arts with criminal intent. One particular sub-faction within Chan's followers was fixated with revenge against Cheung Lai Chuen and plotted his demise.

A few weeks after his victory, Cheung Lai Chuen went for a haircut and shave at a local barber shop that he had never been to before. As he was getting his haircut, the barber - who happened to be from the lineage of Chan Sau, began to express his disgust about how his grandmaster had been defeated by this "Cheung Lai Chuen character." Cheung remained silent and cautiously listened to the barber's tirade, never giving away who he was.

"Who the hell is *he*?!" the barber would interject every so often as he sharpened the straight-edged razor to shave Cheung's neck. "If he were here... I just wish he were here," he continued, waving his blade in a forceful slicing manner.

"Hey, hey, take it easy," Cheung said, "I don't want you to cut *my* neck by accident."

"Oh, oh, I'm sorry," the barber replied, "I got a little carried away. But, I'll kill this Cheung Lai Chuen if I ever meet him!"

Cheung remained calm, patiently listening to the barber's grumblings as he shaved Cheung's neck. When the barber finished the haircut, Cheung paid him. As he was about to walk out the door, Cheung turned back and yelled out, "Hey, I'm Cheung Lai Chuen!" The barber, taken aback, grabbed his straight-edged razor and tried to attack Cheung who in turn used *taan ging* (彈勁), or flicking force, sending the barber flying backward several feet. The injured barber did not pursue Cheung.

Following this foiled assassination attempt, Cheung Lai Chuen casually went to the tea parlor for his usual meal and tea. He told everyone at the table of his encounter and how he had skillfully used his technique to repel his attacker. Everyone who listened to the account praised Cheung for his martial ability and commented that they would recommend him to anyone who wanted to learn martial arts.

After he paid for his meal, Cheung headed for the exit. He sensed uneasiness in the air as he opened the door. Suddenly, an attacker lunged at Cheung with a knife. The Pak Mei master instinctively trapped and broke the assailant's arm as he executed chyun sam geuk. As he released the attacker, he looked around to see a massive mob armed with chains, sticks and knives. In his mind, there seemed to be twenty or more assailants ready to rush toward him. Cheung used his trademark phoenix-eye fist to severely injure two opponents closest to him. He then proceeded to use the two wounded attackers as shields from the knife wielding and chain swinging thugs. Cheung released a flurry of phoenix-eye fists and bone-shattering kicks in a whirlwind of fury. According to Cheung himself, he fought feverishly for a full twenty minutes.

When the assailants realized that their losses equaled or outweighed those still standing, they quickly ran away from the scene. Cheung believed that he killed four attackers at the scene and severely injured approximately half of those who were unable to run from the site like the others. It took Cheung two full days to recuperate from his exhausted state. Rather than deal with the extensive explanations and possible imprisonment for the deaths of those assailants, Cheung was harbored by a handful of his students in *Toisan* (台山 ; *Taishan* in Mandarin) – a city in Guangdong, until the situation resolved itself or merely became forgotten. His stay in Toisan lasted two years and he taught many students during his time there. When he was informed that his return was possible, Cheung found his way back to Guangzhou, again, via his students.

The Challenge at Whampoa

Whampoa Military Academy (黃埔軍校) was the most prestigious establishment dedicated to producing the highest caliber of military tacticians in China. Formally founded on June 16, 1924, Whampoa was the brainchild of Dr. Sun Yat Sen and financially funded by aid from the Soviet Union, particularly during its construction from 1924-1925. Well-known administrators included Chiang Kai-shek (蔣介石) – the academy's first principal and Zhou Enlai (周恩來) – political instructor. Officers and cadets were of an elite class since the academy only recruited the finest candidates in both intelligence and combative expertise. In some instances, members of this privileged group also maintained elitist sentiments – they were selected as the best; hence, they were the best.

After defeating Colonel Liu Chun Fan who went on to become Cheung's first official disciple, Cheung Lai Chuen was highly recommended for a position as combat instructor at the academy. However, Cheung was never formally educated and could not meet the academic requirements to assume such an official position. During an interview, a particular general did not believe that a "country bumpkin" like Cheung could possess such fighting skills.

"What can you do against a gun?" the general asked Cheung in front of his troop of soldiers who were told to be at ease to observe the assessment. "How good is your Kung Fu against a gun?" Cheung merely smiled. The two men continued to exchange words in a very cautious and well-phrased dialogue that was laced with double meaning – they were very kind and polite on the surface, but were filled with adrenaline and readiness beneath. "Why don't we see then?" Cheung finally replied.

"Good!" said the general. "I will leave my gun in its holster and draw it upon the signal to start."

"You should have your gun out now," Cheung responded.

"Ha! No one is that fast, especially from that far away!" mocked the general.

The two men were approximately 10 feet apart. To make the test even more interesting, Cheung requested that the general himself command the countdown to the showdown rather than the judge. The general snickered at the comment and obliged Cheung's invitation, confident that no one's reflexes were that fast. The Pak Mei master nodded.

At the general's signal, both men reacted. The general reached for his gun; Cheung swiftly used *fu bou* (虎步) – the tiger stepping method, toward the general, trapping his opponent's own hand on top of his holster with the gun still in it. Cheung's other hand was positioned by the general's neck, ready to strike with the technique called *bui gim* (背劍), back sword. The general was both surprised and wholly impressed with the speed and precision of Cheung's technique. The cadets were equally amazed and praised Cheung's skill.

Although Cheung could not be a commissioned officer, civilian positions were created to accommodate highly qualified fighting instructors at the academy. This enabled *Lam Yiu Gwai* (林耀桂) – founder of modern-day Lung Ying Kyun, and *Lam Yam Tong* (林蔭堂) – famed Mok Ga exponent, to also teach at the academy due to their extensive experience in combative situations. This trio of skilled experts was dubbed: *Donggong Saam Fu* (東江三虎) – Donggong's Three Tigers, the military academy's designation for the top three fighters from this region of Guangdong Province.

Authentication

In Hong Kong during the 1950s, the pervasive presence of gang members made it extremely difficult for a male teenager to grow up free from violent encounters or unsolicited intrusions. Moreover, the cultural climate tended to reinforce these conditions, leaving few opportunities for teens to escape from illegal influences and criminal activities. Alignment with one gang or members of an organization meant opposition to another; yet, no allegiance was nearly an impossible feat. Kwong Man Fong (鄺文爌) grew up in this very harsh environment as a teenager.

Kwong and his future brother-in-law, Ah Wah, were walking along the streets one day in Hong Kong when three street punks intentionally blocked their paths. The hoodlums then harassed Ah Wah and Kwong for bumping into them and demanded apologies. After an exchange of words and rising tensions, Ah Wah used waan da to strike one of the thugs in the face and Kwong used sip geuk to kick another of the antagonists in the ribs.

The third thug yelled out, "Do you know who we are, you idiots?!"

"I don't care! You deserve it!" Kwong shouted back.

"I know where you live! You're going to pay for this!" the hoodlum screamed out as he went to help his cohorts. Kwong and Ah Wah casually walked away.

Later that day when Kwong and Ah Wah were practicing their Pak Mei on their rooftop, they heard a car come to a screeching halt on the street below. Then, they heard another… and another, until four vehicles lined the streets below with gang members dashing out from them.

"Hey!! Come down here, you coward!" the youth that Kwong kicked yelled out. "You better come down or we're going to burn your house down!"

Ah Wah was petrified. Kwong told Ah Wah to stay on the roof as he picked up his staff, broke off the blade of a knife and tucked it into the waistband of his pants. Ah Wah remained on the roof. As Kwong was coming down the stairs, a few of the gang members were coming up. In the ensuing excitement, one of the lead members charged at Kwong. He was struck on the head by Kwong's staff. Kwong then quickly rushed past him and the others making his way onto the street so that Ah Wah would be spared.

When Kwong appeared outside, the gang members were waiting for him with chains, knives, sticks and anything else that could be used for a weapon since guns were illegal in Hong Kong.

"Who do you think you are to do this to my brother!" the leader yelled out to Kwong.

"Look, I didn't want any trouble! But, they wouldn't let us pass," Kwong explained.

A few more exchanges were made until Kwong finally said, "Look, I'll fight all of you, just not here. Let's go to the waterfront."

All agreed. When they arrived at the waterfront, the leader said to Kwong, "You must know something [Kung Fu] to act the way that you do. What style do you practice?"

Kwong responded pompously, "Pak Mei."

"Bull!" the leader yelled back angrily. "*We* are Pak Mei Paai!" he continued, thumbing toward his chest.

Kwong smiled.

"Who's your teacher?!" the leader demanded. "Who's your teacher?!"

"Ha," Kwong mocked, "Cheung Lai Chuen."

"You're lying!" the leader hollered at Kwong. "My sifu is 6th generation Pak Mei Paai. That would make you my si suk!"

Kwong shook his head, "No, that would make me your *si suk gung*."

The gangsters refused to believe Kwong, but they were also at a stalemate in trying to resolve the situation.

"OK, if you don't believe me, come to the tea parlor tomorrow morning, if you have the guts. I will introduce you to *my* sifu," Kwong said.

The leader stood silent. "Alright, but if you're not there, consider yourself dead."

The next morning, Kwong waited for the gang leader in addition to his usual wait for Cheung Lai Chuen.

The gangster arrived first.

Kwong thought to himself, "Great, what a day for sifu not to show up."

The gang leader saw Kwong without his teacher and began to strut arrogantly toward him. As the gangster approached Kwong to tell him that he and his cousin were dead, Cheung Lai Chuen walked into the tea house. "Perfect timing," Kwong thought to himself.

"Sifu, wai, sifu!" Kwong yelled out very noticeably. Cheung Lai Chuen acknowledged Kwong with a nod. "Come meet my teacher," Kwong said proudly – and relieved, "I'll introduce you to him."

The hoodlum quickly turned away and walked briskly out the tea parlor.

"Ah Yiu, who was that?" Cheung asked Kwong.

"Sifu, he said he didn't believe that I learned from you," Kwong said.

"What?! Who the hell is he?" Cheung demanded to know.

Kwong explained the entire incident to his teacher during their morning tea.

"I'll talk to his teacher, that disrespectful worm," Cheung told Kwong.

Later on that same day, the gang leader came to meet Kwong at Kwong's building.

"Ok, so that's your teacher. You still need to give face to my brother for kicking him so hard though," the gangster said, reaching for a reason to remain above Kwong.

Kwong took out twenty dollars and said, "Here, give this to your brother so that he can get some dit da treatment for his bruise."

"Oh, hey no, that's OK," the hoodlum changed his tone, slipping in the opportunity to recruit Kwong, "I mean, we are in fact all part of the *same family*, right?"

"No!" Kwong quickly responded, realizing what the gangster was trying to do. "We are *not* the same [referring to gangster activities and affiliated membership through Pak Mei Kung Fu]. When you see me, don't even acknowledge that you know me. I am not you!"

At that, the gangster smirked and left, never to see Kwong again.

Final Reflections

While there are numerous stories and variations that have been passed down about Cheung Lai Chuen's exploits from different teachers, there are consistent themes that recur about the great master.

Whereas titles such as fearless, courageous, and resolute are routinely used to describe Cheung's spirit, terms such as sensitive, kind or compassionate are typically absent from depictions of his personality. Cheung Lai Chuen was an intense individual. Being at the top and staying at the top among an entire province's martial exponents was a challenge that molded his outlook and shaped his reservations. Combative confrontations awaited him everywhere and trustworthy allies were scarce. To Cheung, everyone wanted something from him; otherwise, they would not dare to deal with him. Consequently, he had very little regard or patience for those who did not have the ability to learn from him – and even less for those who were merely acquainted with him.

As with any other individual, Cheung Lai Chuen was a product of his time. There were circumstances that enabled him to be considered great, and there were situations that forced him to be detached. This can be said of anyone who has had the opportunity to be considered great within his/her lifetime. With Cheung Lai Chuen, being one of the greatest martial exponents of his time and region, and propagating a martial method that had not been publicly taught prior to him were his primary objectives. His accomplishments speak for themselves, and his martial descendants maintain his martial legacy in the times in which they themselves live.

About The Author

Williy Pang has over 30 years of interest and experience in Chinese martial arts with nearly 20 years dedicated to Pak Mei Kung Fu. Several of his articles focused on Pak Mei Kung Fu have been featured in Kung Fu Tai Chi Magazine.

He resides in New York City.

TNP MULTIMEDIA LLC

also presents

Pak Mei Kung Fu:

The Myth & The Martial Art

by S. L. Fung

ISBN: 978-0-9814813-0-2

Pak Mei Kung Fu:

Southern Style Staff

by Williy Pang

ISBN: 978-0-9814813-1-9

Available @ www.nypakmei.com